LINCOLN CHRISTIAN COLLEGE AND SEMINARY

W9-BKB-031

WALKING THROUGH THE VALLEY

*Understanding and Emerging
from Clergy Depression*

LINCOLN CHRISTIAN COLLEGE AND SEMINARY

WALKING THROUGH THE VALLEY

Understanding and Emerging from Clergy Depression

ROBERT L. RANDALL
FOREWORD BY JAMES B. NELSON

ABINGDON PRESS
Nashville

WALKING THROUGH THE VALLEY
UNDERSTANDING AND EMERGING FROM CLERGY DEPRESSION

Copyright © 1998 by Abingdon Press

All rights reserved.
No part of this work may be reproduced or transmitted in any form or by any means, electronic or mechanical, including photocopying and recording, or by any infor-mation storage or retrieval system, except as may be expressly permitted by the 1976 Copyright Act or in writing from the publisher. Requests for permission should be addressed in writing to Abingdon Press, P.O. Box 801, 201 Eighth Avenue South, Nashville, TN 37202-0801.

This book is printed on recycled, acid-free, elemental-chlorine-free paper.

ISBN 0-687-014638

Library of Congress Cataloging-in-Publication Data

Randall, Robert L., 1942–
    Walking through the valley: understanding and emerging from clergy depression/Robert L. Randall: foreword by James B. Nelson.
        p.   cm.
    Includes bibliographical references.
    ISBN 0-687-01463-8 (pbk.: alk. paper)
        1. Clergy—Psychology.   2. Depression, Mental.   I. Title.
BV4398.R35   1998
253'.2—dc21   97-42421
                                                               CIP

Unless otherwise noted, Scripture quotations are from the New Revised Standard Version Bible. Copyright © 1989 by the Division of Christian Education of the National Council of the Churches of Christ in the USA. Used by permission.

Scripture quotations noted KJV are from the King James version of the Bible.

Psalms/Now by Leslie Brandt, Copyright 1973 Concordia Publishing House. Adapted by permission.

Excerpt from the English translation of *The Liturgy of the Hours* © 1974, International Committee on English in the Liturgy, Inc. All rights reserved.

98 99 00 01 02 03 04 05 06 07—10 9 8 7 6 5 4 3 2 1

MANUFACTURED IN THE UNITED STATES OF AMERICA

ACKNOWLEDGMENTS

Good friends are a joy. They are also wonderful anti-depressants. In our journey through life, what helps us through the valleys is not where we've been or what we own but who we have beside us.

I'm grateful for two dear friends who have sustained me for years and now have contributed to this book. James B. Nelson makes my heart sing with his foreword, as he did when I was a student in his class. Those of you who have met Dr. Nelson as he speaks about "embodiment" and about men's issues know what a warm and insightful person he is. Thank you, Jim, for so very much.

I've relied upon my old seminary roommate, the Reverend Larry Randen, to preview each chapter. Besides being a scholar in religious myth and symbolism, he has a wonderful capacity for editorial work. Thank you, Larry, for years of "looking me over."

93365

CONTENTS

FOREWORD

For many years I have followed Robert L. Randall's distinguished career as pastoral counselor, scholar, and author with admiration and gratitude. So it is a particular delight to write the foreword to this latest book by a friend and former student.

It is, as we have come to expect from him, an eminently understandable and useful book, useful for the pastor's own self-appraisal and for the care of others. Dr. Randall guides us through the diagnosis of depression, determining its depth and seriousness and addressing its causes. Though he writes with nontechnical clarity, he never sacrifices his nuanced and experienced understanding of the disease's complexities.

Similarly, charting the paths of recovery, Randall lucidly develops the stages through which healing typically passes. He claims neither too little nor too much. He does not oversimplify the healing of this complex disease. Yet, with ample illustration and memorable images—"applying the brakes, holding still, returning home, and stepping beyond"—Randall moves us through the processes necessary for recovery.

I want to comment on several issues raised by this important book. The first has to do with *men* and depression. Randall, very appropriately, writes with gender inclusiveness in both language and subject matter. Clergy who suffer from depression are both female and male, and the author's illustrations are rooted in his counseling experience with both sexes. At the same time, I think there are reasons to draw attention to some present gender differences in this disease.

It is commonplace for those of us immersed in the men's movement to observe how the cultural socialization of males still encourages us to filter our feelings of self-esteem through performance and achievement, and how our shaping encourages us to stifle a whole range of feelings that we perceive as unmasculine. If women tend more to blame themselves for their pain, we men tend to feel victimized by others. As a result we may strike out with antisocial behavior or mask those urges in addictions. And because men so frequently perceive depression as unmanly and shameful, and are still chronically less inclined to ask for help, it is no surprise that we are several times more likely than women to kill ourselves. In a word, depression in men is often difficult to detect, but it is terribly real and distressingly common. Nevertheless, once depression is diagnosed, the promises of effective therapy and possibilities of recovery are very hopeful, indeed.

While I pray for the day when gender justice will have erased the differences in both numbers and power between clergymen and clergywomen, and I yearn for the day when male socialization patterns will be less emotionally destructive, that day is not yet here. Thus, I find this important book taking on a particular urgency for men. I think that is worth emphasis.

Three themes in Randall's understanding of depression and its healing engaged me in especially personal ways: the significance of the body, our distinctly human power to create our own patterns of meaning, and depression as a potentially transforming event. The themes have intertwined in my own experience.

Illness and its healing are always *embodied* experiences. This is no less true of depression than of cancer, even though the former is commonly seen as an emotional and not a physical malady. One of the most destructive heresies in much Christian thought through the ages has been the divorce between body and spirit. But that divorce is a broadly cultural problem as well as a religious one, and it has deeply affected (and infected) modern Western medicine. One of Randall's many gifts in this book is his clear grasp of the biophysical factors in both depression's causation and its healing. Furthermore, worries about the body, preoccupation with the body, loss of energy and vitality, suicidal thoughts or attempts—all can be bodily manifestations and signals of serious illness, surely including depression.

I found *Walking Through the Valley* enormously helpful for understanding my own valley experience. I have been in recovery from alcoholism for several years, and have given much thought to that disease. Until reading this book, however, I had not been aware of the extent to which depression likely was a part of my illness—as it frequently is. From the vantage point of recovery, I can also recognize how profoundly the whole embodied self is implicated in both of these diseases. As in depression, biophysical factors are contributing causes in alcoholism, too. But body wisdom, when heard and understood, can also be an effective ally in curbing the disease. Had my denial not so effectively stilled the messages my body was sending (and which in retrospect I can now clearly identify), I would have sought treatment earlier than I did.

I also know something of the importance and promise of Randall's insight about wrestling a blessing from the disease. To be sure, when certain diseases are still moralized with blame and shame, the blessing may be difficult to find. Such is often still true of both depression and alcoholism. But with such diseases, as the author makes utterly clear, simple recovery is not enough. It is not enough just to get back to where we were before the disease began to take hold. No, our hope and our possibilities are larger—a different life, transformed by a power greater than ours. That is the blessing.

11

But everything depends upon interpretation. How we respond to anything depends upon our interpretation of its meaning for us. Randall rightly emphasizes that we have the awesome capacity literally to create our worlds of meaning, a capacity that reflects the *imago dei* we bear. Transformations of our life, furthermore, rest upon this capacity to generate new patterns of meaning.

Years ago H. Richard Niebuhr taught us that while Christian ethics has often been interpreted as either an ethics of goal-seeking or an ethics of obedience, a more adequate pattern is that of *responsibility*. This means the ability to respond fittingly to events by interpreting the activity of God in the midst of them. It does not imply that God has caused specific events to happen as they do. Such interpretations would deny both human freedom and divine justice. Events such as illnesses are not divinely produced. They are caused by combinations of finite factors, but God is still in their midst with a creative presence yearning for some kind of healing, for the reordering of life, for empowerment, for transformation—in short, for blessing. To see that presence and to respond to it in the midst of our experiences can make all the difference in the world.

For many years at some level I had believed this to be true. And I had attempted to live this way, trying to see the divine presence and meanings in the midst of human events. However, it was not until I became willing to deal with the crisis of my alcoholism and its attendant depression that I realized the enormous power of both unfaithful and faithful patterns of interpretation. Part of the reason for my illness was a pattern of false interpretation of reality, and that untruth was making me seriously ill. But recognizing and dealing with my illness, finally being forced to honor it, "fractured the habituality" of my thinking, in the author's words. It jarred me to see and respond to God in ways I had not before.

For example, in one of the first lectures that I heard at the Hazelden Center where I had gone for treatment, the speaker said, "You might think I'm crazy when I say this, but some day you will be grateful for your alcoholism." My initial reaction was, "You are perfectly right. I believe you are crazy. Grateful for treatment? Yes. Grateful for hope? Yes. But grateful for the *disease*? No, thank you!" In the strange economy of God, however, I have begun now to see things differently.

Surely, it has been a process, and it is far from finished. But Randall is right, I am convinced, in saying that however much we loathe our disease we must honor it. We must honor and not deny its reality and power. We must honor its "personhood," for the disease affects the totality of our being and everything we touch. And we can honor, with gratitude, its potential. Though God surely has not caused this, by responding to the divine presence in the midst of this, life can be transformed. Priorities can be reordered, self-understandings altered, behaviors changed, the embodied experience of the sacred expanded, the permeation of daily life by God made more real. In Robert Randall's eminently fitting words, the disease has become "a crucible for new life in part through our ability to integrate it into our life-story in transforming ways." And that integration comes, I believe, when we begin to see our own life-stories through the stories that the church tells about God.

James B. Nelson
Professor Emeritus of Christian Ethics
United Theological Seminary of the Twin Cities

INTRODUCTION

Honoring Our Depression

*Even though I walk through the valley
of the shadow of death, I fear no evil.*
Psalm 23:4 *(alternate reading)*

Opening this book is a sign of hope. If you are depressed, it indicates that you have energy left to help yourself. If you are attempting to prevent depression, or to minimize depression should it come, it signifies that you have the resource of wisdom. If you are endeavoring to help a depressed pastor, opening this book shows that an environment of care still surrounds that pastor, and that you have the courage to face depression's toxicity.

When depressed clergy come to me for counseling, I tell them they face four renewal tasks. The first is to *apply brakes.* We need to stop their downward skid. The next task is to *hold still.* They need to catch their breath, to convalesce for a while at the point at which they stopped their decline. The next task is to *return home.* This is the road back to their previously normal state.

This should not be the final destination, however. I suggest that the next task is to *step beyond.* It is not enough, it is not a valid taxation of our spirit, to be yanked through the hell of depression only to resurface at the spot we left. *We should wrestle a blessing from depression.* We should strive to make our depression make us better than what we were. As depression transforms us into forms of ourselves we despise,

15

so must we labor to make depression transform us into forms of ourselves we desire: more peaceful selves, more courageous selves, more understanding selves.

This book, based on my thirty years of counseling depressed pastors and their families,[1] is dedicated to accomplishing these renewal tasks. Its aim is to help us clergy survive our depression. More than that, through God's grace it attempts to help us clergy transform our pain into insight and our struggles into expansions of our spirit.

However much we might loathe our depression, wisdom dictates that we honor it. We clergy are not very good at this.

In the first place, we should honor depression's presence. Depression in some form is epidemic among clergy, and appears to be increasing. Most of us clergy will at some time experience depression, whether mild or severe.

And yet our grandiosity tends to keep us clergy from owning up to our depression or its possibility. We deny or minimize our depression, on the one hand, because admitting our depression is a blow to our self-esteem. Being depressed is taken as weakness, and admitting our weakness injures our esteem. Better to hurt than to acknowledge ourselves as human.

Even when the signs of depression are inescapable, we flinch from having it recognized. One pastor for whom medication had been prescribed said this: "As I stood in line at the pharmacy waiting to get my antidepressant, I felt a great wave of shame spread over me. The person behind the counter would know what I was getting. I felt embarrassed to be seen as 'depressed.' In spite of how miserable I'd been, I was tempted to forget the prescription and continue on rather than be mortified."[2]

Little wonder, then, that when I ask pastors to indicate where they are on a hypothetical scale from 0 to 10, with 0 being no depression at all and 10 the worst possible case of depression, they tend to rate themselves low. One pastor commented, "Well, I'd like to think I'm at a zero, but I suppose after what we've talked about I'm probably at a two or three." In actuality he was much higher on the scale than that.

The denial or minimizing of our depression is sustained, on the other hand, by the grandiose myths parishioners tend to whisper in our ear, such as, "You are so strong and confident"; "You work so hard and do so much"; "You possess such remarkable faith." We either buy into these myths and thus disavow our depression, or else we are reluctant to ruin the image others have of us. Consequently we experience fatigue, irritation, and the erosion of our spirit, but rationalize that we are too strong, too smart, or too successful to be afflicted with real depression.

In the second place, we should honor depression's power. Depression in any form inhibits our functioning. It devours our pleasure. It tempts us toward activities that are more harmful than restorative. It seduces us, at times, to entertain thoughts of killing ourselves.

Nevertheless, when we're depressed we clergy carry on as if we're not a danger to ourselves or to anyone else. The fact is that in becoming depressed we become "at risk" caregivers. "At risk" means we are in such a vulnerable state that we tend to "act-in" or "act-out."

In acting-in we internalize feelings, thoughts, and reactions. We keep everything inside—stewing, denying, rationalizing, raging. The result is restlessness, sleeplessness, hopelessness, physical problems, and suicide inclinations. Tensions mount without release or resolve.

In acting-out we externalize our feelings, thoughts, and reactions. We keep everything outside—blaming, arguing, or manipulating to the point where we interact with others in destructive ways. The all-too-familiar crossing of boundaries some clergy commit, such as betrayal of confidences or sexual improprieties, often stem from ministers who are struggling with depression. When we fail to honor depression's power, we are even more at risk to others and ourselves.

In the third place, we clergy should honor depression's potential. The message of history, from biblical figures to current Christians, is that through the experience of depression we can become more understanding human beings. Without glorifying suffering, or espousing a "no pain, no gain" philosophy, individuals can affirm depression's potential for stimulating growth.

We clergy, however, tend to vilify depression. We make our depression "the enemy" we must defeat. We use the swords of intensified work, self-directed anger, or stiff drinks to slay "the dark beast" whenever we see it raise its ominous head.

This is understandable. Whatever hurts us does seem malicious. Furthermore, when we're in pain our capacities weaken for seeing good possibilities.

Depression, however, can be a crucible for new life. Our depression can prompt us to healthier behavior. It can become a condition for knowing what is true and valuable. It can deepen our empathy for others and for ourselves. One pastor who, like the psalmists, had found enlightenment on the other side of depression thanked God for "the gifts of this dark angel."

Finally, in the fourth place, we clergy should honor depression's personhood. Depression is a "person" condition. Our self is involved. Depression does not just *affect* us; it *is* us. Depression arises, in part, from within us, by the ways we have dealt with the world and related to others. Its course and intensity are shaped, in part, by our mental, emotional, and physical inclinations. Depression lifts, in part, as we reorganize our lived situations, central meanings, and bodily functions. Depression becomes a crucible for new life in part through our ability to integrate it into our life-story in transforming ways.

Nonetheless, we clergy tend to regard depression as a disease that has invaded us. We're inclined to consider ourselves primarily as patients who must be treated. We focus on getting rid of the illness. We react as if we were victims.

This is understandable, too. We don't want to be the way we are. We do feel invaded. The medical world now rightly proclaims to us that depression is an illness, often involving some chemical deficiency. The social world is beginning to rightly proclaim that depression is not a character deficiency, something for which we are morally responsible.

The unfortunate result of these correct emphases is to *depersonalize* depression. We are lured into viewing depression merely in terms of processes and mechanisms that happen to us. We are seduced into treating depression as if we had diabetes or cancer. But although medical interventions are helpful, even necessary at times, depression is ultimately a *self* disturbance. We need to stand up to depression but not depersonalize it.

Good pastoral care always begins with pastoral assessment. We clergy do that with parishioners and their problems. We should do it with ourselves and our depression. Chapter 1, therefore, begins by diagnosing our depression. Such an effort helps us determine whether we have depression or not, what kind we have if we do, what we are up against, and how we might best respond in light of the basic characteristics of depression.

In facing our depression, we pastors often know how badly we feel but not how bad we are. We look for some measure of how seriously affected we've become. Chapter 2, therefore, describes a range of "levels of self-disturbance" generated by depression. These levels are also instructive for those who want to know how to respond to depressed clergy.

We clergy also yearn for explanations that will make sense of our condition. Chapter 3 addresses that yearning by describing "the depression triangle." Every occurrence of depression involves the interlocking of situation, meaning, and body.

Chapter 4 highlights the four renewal tasks. This concept of renewal tasks grew out of years of watching the normal course of depression in pastors I counseled. Their downward spiral typically stopped at some level. They lingered for a time at this point. They began the process of returning to normal. Following this, some moved on to reshape their lives. Pastors and I simply try to help this healing course along. We work to *apply brakes*, to *hold still*, to *return home*, and to *step beyond*.

Chapter 5 specifically addresses the renewal task of *applying brakes*. Suggestions for how to apply brakes with situations, meanings, and bodily processes are given. Similarly, chapter 6 focuses on *holding still* and how to do this with the triangle of situation, meaning, and body. Chapters 7 and 8 do the same for the tasks of *returning home* and *stepping beyond*.

Our goal is to "walk through the valley." That journey begins with the affirmation of faith stated in our opening verse: "Even though . . ." Our depression is not our destiny. It is not the ultimate power. In a spirit of "even though," we look through our depression toward the other side: *Even though things are not going well with me, God is at work in every breath and movement.* With that belief as a friend to our heart we walk concerned but not afraid.

CHAPTER ONE

Diagnosing Our Depression

Good pastoral care always begins with pastoral assessment. Although we feel lousy, it's important to make sure we're depressed rather than suffering from some other ailment. Furthermore, possessing knowledge about depression is a step toward regaining our sense of control—which we often lose when depressed.[1]

DEPRESSION IS DISTINCTIVE

Depression is a mood disorder. It has specific symptoms that set it apart from other ailments. The signs of depression are these:

Persistent sad/empty mood
Loss of interest in pleasurable activities
Decreased energy; fatigue
Decreased ability to concentrate, remember, decide
Negative or pessimistic attitude
Feelings of helplessness, worthlessness, hopelessness
Suicide thoughts or attempts; preoccupation with death
Sleep disturbance (too little or too much)
Eating disturbance (too little or too much)

A person is said to be clinically depressed when five or more of these symptoms are present. These symptoms *as a cluster* are specific for depression. They are not found in other emotional disturbances.

When we clergy, like others, are upset, we tend to report a general distress. We do not usually differentiate between depressive symptoms and symptoms of other emotional disturbances. A specific diagnosis of depression, however, is important for determining causes, impact, and treatment.

Other symptoms often associated with depression are: headaches, constipation, vague abdominal pains, and neck tension. Anxiety may or may not be present. The same is true about anger. These latter two are not used to diagnose the presence or absence of depression.

Three basic types of depression have been identified. They are determined by the severity and duration of symptoms. They are called mild depression, major depression, and dys-thymia (dis-thim' e-ah).

Mild depression:	mild symptoms/short duration
Major depression:	moderate to severe symptoms/ short duration
Dysthymia:	mild symptoms/long duration

Mild depression is not "the blues" that hit all of us peri-odically. It is more like a state of deep melancholy. Five or more of the depression symptoms will last *less* than two weeks.

In major depression the symptoms are moderate to severe. The duration is also short but will last a minimum of two weeks. A specific event often triggers this type of depression. It occurs most commonly in adulthood.

With dysthymia the symptoms are mild but the duration is longer: *at least* two years. No easily recognized event triggers this depression. It tends to begin in childhood and adolescence but recurs in adulthood. Because of its long duration, dysthymia is often more detrimental than major depression. Studies show that 79 percent of dysthymic indi-

viduals eventually develop a major depression, thus quali-
fying for a diagnosis of "double depression."

There is a condition called manic-depression in which
episodes of despondency alternate with episodes of frantic
behavior. Strictly speaking this is a bipolar disorder distinct
from depressive disorders. Although it certainly occurs in
the lives of clergy, we will not be considering it in this book.

Implications for clergy:
1. Chart your symptoms, along with their severity and
   duration, if you think you may be depressed.
2. Compare your current feelings with similar feelings
   you might have had in the past and note what happened in the past.
3. Ask a loved one or person who knows you well how
   they currently perceive you.
4. Spend money for at least an assessment interview with
   a pastoral counselor, psychologist, social worker, or
   psychiatrist skilled in diagnosing depression.

DEPRESSION IS SELF-LIMITING

In all likelihood, we depressed clergy will eventually get
better—even without medication or therapy. Unlike other
conditions, which may linger for a lifetime without substan-
tial change (chronic anxiety, obsessive-compulsions, pho-
bias, paranoia), depression has a limited duration. Even in
severe situations, depression usually lifts in six months to
two years.

Implications for clergy:
1. Don't panic when you become depressed. Getting better is possible, even likely.
2. Take a *working it through* attitude. Cooperate with the
   healing process rather than fight it.

Depression Is Dangerous

Although self-limiting, depression is dangerous. It can be lethal.

- About 15 percent of those depressed commit suicide. Even mildly depressed persons may commit suicide.
- More males *commit* suicide than females. More females *attempt* suicide than males.
- Most suicide victims are aged fifty and older.
- More white males commit suicide than nonwhite males.
- More single people commit suicide than married people.
- People suffering from alcoholism have a much greater chance of committing suicide than those without this disease.

Depression is erosive. Our relationships become inevitably injured to some degree. Unhealthy efforts to deal with our depression, such as drinking, sexual affairs, impulsive changing of churches, or relinquishing of our pastoral leadership, undercut our integrity. Physical ailments may also arise. In short, our depressive symptoms may go away but their negative consequences often linger.

Depression is contagious. Others become susceptible to depression when exposed to our depression.

Depression is exorbitant. Work is missed or attended to only marginally. Treatment for depression can be costly. Other related problems, such as physical ailments, poor money decisions, and marital breakups may be financially draining.

Depression can be chronic. Especially when our depression is linked with other emotional conditions, our depression may linger on. Recovery may be incomplete.

Implications for clergy:

1. Take any thought, rumination, or idea you might have about death/suicide very seriously. Talk to someone about it—now!
2. Make no major financial, career, relationship, or other significant decision when depressed.
3. Warn loved ones to keep healthy boundaries between their emotions and your emotions lest they, too, become depressed.
4. Make up your mind to spend money to overcome your depression, or to prevent more serious depression, rather than having to spend it on the devastating results of depression.
5. Work to resolve your emotional problems as they arise so that if you become depressed in the future, unresolved problems will not exacerbate the effects of your depression.

DEPRESSION IS SELECTIVE

Most depressed individuals are between 25 and 44 years of age. Depression is two to three times more likely to strike those with a family history of depression. Depression tends to hit those who are already down. Depression afflicts twice as many women as it does men.

Implications for clergy:

1. Do not think that depression is an old age disease to which your more youthful mind and body are immune. Note that age 25 is about when most seminarians begin their ministry, age 25 through 44 is when clergy try to make their mark, and age 44 is about the time female clergy begin their menopause.

2. Take seriously a history of depression in your family as a factor in diagnosing and working through your depression.
3. At all times try to strengthen and protect your mind, body, relationships, and spirit. These, too, are antidepressants.
4. As pastors, let us be aware of, and responsive to, the reality that female clergy are at a high risk for depression.

Depression Is Epidemic

Each year more than 11 million Americans are affected by depression. One in four women, and one in ten men, will experience at least one debilitating episode of depression during their lifetime.

Depression is also increasing. Those born after World War II are more likely to experience depression than their forebears.

Implications for clergy:
1. Preach and teach about the prevalence of depression. Your effort to alert others will aid them as well as yourself as you stay active in facing your depression.
2. Pray specifically about the depressed state of individuals rather than pray generally that they recover from their problems. Naming depression as a reality is a step toward overcoming it.
3. Work to eliminate those conditions that give rise to unnecessary depression.

Depression Is Treatable

Up to 90 percent of individuals can be helped with psychotherapy, antidepressants, ECT (electroconvulsive therapy), or a combination of these. Depression, however, is undertreated. Because of fear or ignorance, up to 50 percent of depressed individuals seek no treatment. When help is sought, health providers frequently misdiagnose or pass over depressive symptoms. Even when a proper diagnosis of depression is made, 20 percent to 50 percent or more of depressed individuals do not comply with recommenda- tions for outpatient therapy. Even when highly motivated middle-class persons do enter outpatient therapy, over a third drop out of insight-oriented psychotherapy prema- turely. Likewise, antidepressive medication is often not taken as prescribed. In about 75 percent of studies with depressed persons, however, social support from others has been found to increase the initial success of treatment and to help persons maintain the achievements they make in treat- ment.

Implications for clergy:
1. Consult a health provider to help you with your de- pression, particularly one skilled in the diagnosis and treatment of depression.
2. Do not hesitate to interview several providers in the search for someone to work with you.
3. Make competency the first criterion when choosing a provider and feeling comfortable the second. Your comfort with a provider may mean he or she is failing to adequately confront you with the realities of your depression.
4. Do not hesitate to get a second opinion if your provider suggests a treatment that is puzzling or frightening to you.
5. Once you have checked out the proposed treatment plan, follow it to completion.
6. Find and maintain a support group while going through treatment. Having a hand to hold is excellent medicine.

DEPRESSION IS MIMICKED

Physical illnesses are great mimickers of emotional disorders. Thus, not everything that looks like depression is depression. Persons in the first stages of cancer show symptoms similar to depression. Their problem, however, is not emotional but physical. Other physical illnesses that commonly give rise to depression-like symptoms are: estrogen imbalances, diabetes, and thyroid problems.

Implications for clergy:
1. Consider physiological illness as a possible cause of your depressive symptoms.
2. Be receptive to the use of physical exams and lab work to rule out the presence of a medical disease.
3. Request physical exams and lab work if your depression persists after being treated by psychotherapy and/or antidepressants.

DEPRESSION IS CONTROVERSIAL

For most of this century, depression was considered a character defect. Depression represented a weakness in the personality. In 1980 this diagnosis was radically rethought. In professional circles depression is now understood to be a mood disturbance rather than a personality defect.

And yet today 50 percent of Americans still think of depression as a character deficiency. Pastors themselves tend to regard their own depression with embarrassment. The very evidence of their depression lowers their already low self-esteem.

Clergy and others have attitudinal changes to make. They are responsible for responding to their depression, but they are not totally responsible for the rise of their depression. Biochemical changes in the body, inherited dispositions, and natural depletion when faced with stresses argue against seeing depression as a character weakness.

There are also controversies over medication. Antidepressant medication continues to be the most common treatment for depression in the United States. Thoughtful reservations can be raised about its use, however.

- If depression is also mental and spiritual in nature, shouldn't it be dealt with without medication?
- Isn't there an ethical dilemma in giving medication to a depressed individual to help him or her endure a situation that really should be changed?
- Aren't there studies showing that psychotherapy alone is as effective as medication alone, and even as effective as the combination of psychotherapy and medication?
- Since 70 percent of all antidepressant medications are prescribed for women, isn't there a danger that they will be disproportionately subject to the side effects and risk of these medications?
- Isn't there the risk that antidepressants may encourage dependency, passivity, and a victim psychology in women, and thus reinforce their depression over time?

Antidepressant medication, however, is extremely valuable. When administered thoughtfully and skillfully, along with counseling, it can aid the resurrection of our spirit. As one depressed pastor said, "Antidepressants help my body sustain who I am." She knew, from experience, that the medication did not make her something other than what she was. She also knew, from experience, that the medication helped preserve something of utmost importance: her very self. Antidepressants helped her body function in order to sustain her personality.

Medication does not solve problems but rather aids in coping with problems. As another pastor taking antidepressants said, "I still feel in the dark, but I'm no longer in a deep hole in the dark. That makes a big difference."

The place of ECT (electroconvulsive therapy) is also highly controversial. For less than a second, low levels of current are passed through electrodes attached to both of a person's temples. Since muscle-relaxing medication is given prior to treatment, there is hardly any movement of the individual's body. No discomfort is felt. The person does not remember the procedure, which may be repeated several times on different days. After several treatments there is some memory impairment that lasts from one to several weeks after the last treatment.

Calling ECT "shock therapy" conjures up frightening images. No one really knows how ECT works. Some argue that ECT brings recovery but with a risk of brain damage and permanent memory loss. A few states have outlawed ECT for individuals under a certain age.

Sometimes, however, psychotherapy and medication are ineffective. The depressed person seems trapped in profound apathy and hopelessness. ECT can be a helpful treatment in these situations. Pastoral counselor William Hulme, in an account of his own bout with depression, says that ECT was crucial to his recovery and the easiest medical treatment he received.[2] Susan Alloway, writing in *Pastoral Psychology* about her struggle with depression, also states that her depression lifted only through the use of ECT.[3]

Similarly, stroke victims do not become gradually depressed after their stroke but are suddenly in a full-blown major depression as soon as they regain consciousness. Antidepressants and ECT can help them get better. If they do not receive these treatments, their depressed mood lasts from six months to a year or more.

Withholding ECT treatment because of side effects has been compared with prohibiting lifesaving surgery because a patient's skin may be scarred in the process. Used selec-

tively and skillfully, ECT can relieve the burden of depression for the greater good of the individual.

Finally, controversy remains about depression in women.
Women tend to become depressed at an earlier age than men
do. Furthermore, depression actually afflicts twice as many
women as men, although the gap seems to be narrowing.

One argument for why female depression is so prevalent
says that the social roles of women are inherently depressing.
Subservient roles and less acceptance of women's emotions
in the workplace and devalued roles of homemaking lead
women to become more frequently depressed. Men, in con-
trast, do not suffer as much from limited roles and lack of life
choices and are thus less at risk for becoming depressed.

A related argument for the prevalence of female depression says that a woman's core sense of self is more relation-
ally based than a man's. Simultaneously, women are
bombarded by cultural norms, different from those that hit
men, which dictate how they are to be in relationships:
interpersonally sensitive, passive, and accommodating.
Women, therefore, experience a no-win either/or tension in
their lives: either fulfill cultural expectations and sacrifice
their own needs in order to preserve relationships or act on
their own needs and feelings at the risk of losing relationships. The result is more depressed women than men.

A contrasting explanation says that it is not necessary to
show that women are depressed by social roles or by no-win
tensions. It is sufficient to show that *they believe* they are
dependent, helpless, or conflicted. They suffer from a tendency to regard themselves as lacking life choices, and thus
are receptive to becoming depressed. What needs to be
changed are not so much cultural norms and expectations for
women but rather women's own internal views about themselves and society.

My work with depressed women, especially female
clergy, has shown that unique cultural restrictions as well as
cognitive attitudes and biological changes contribute signifi-

cantly to their depression. Causes for their depression are multiple.

We will not attempt to resolve the controversy regarding female depression, or female versus male depression. Our main focus will be on the similarities in the depressions of men and women clergy: similar symptoms (chapter 1), similar levels of self-disturbance (chapter 2), similar general causes (chapter 3), and similar steps to recovery (chapters 4 through 8).

CHAPTER TWO

Determining How Depressed We Are

Reverend Merrill looked down at his hands. "It's easy to say, 'I'm feeling depressed.' Everyone gets that way. No big deal. But it's really hard to say, 'I'm not just *feeling* depressed, I *am* depressed.' That's scary."

It *is* scary. It's hard to look at our symptoms and acknowledge our depression. But facing our depression is also a wise decision. Honoring the presence of depression is a decided step toward working through it.

Besides worrying about *what* we have we worry about *how bad* we have it. We want to know the seriousness of our condition. We usually have a hunch. If we are still in partial denial, however, we may underestimate how depressed we are. If we begin to panic, we may overestimate how depressed we are. Furthermore, since impaired judgment is often a characteristic of depression, our own judgments about our depression may be unreliable.

There's another reason for assessing the level of our depression. We also need to know how strong we are. We need to affirm those capacities which depression has not damaged. These capacities will sustain us in the process of working through our depression.

When counseling depressed clergy, I help them assess the level of their depression in three ways.[1] First, as noted in the introduction, I initially ask them to indicate how depressed they are on a hypothetical scale from 0 to 10. These impressionistic self-reports are used to determine if clergy are truly aware of their depression and have even a ballpark idea of how affected they've become.

Second, we consider the nature of their symptoms: number of symptoms, duration of symptoms, and severity of symptoms. This symptom analysis allows us to distinguish among the categories of mild depression, major depression, and dysthymia. Symptom analysis, however, is more useful in diagnosing the presence and type of depression than in determining the extent of depression.

Third, pastors and I assess the degree to which the cohesion of their self has been disrupted by depression. Depression is an indication that the pastor's self has become seriously fragmented. The symptoms of depression are specific products of this fragmentation. They are signs that the stability of the pastor's self has deteriorated.

LEVELS OF SELF-DISTURBANCE

Depression *affects* our total self. It may not *alter* our total self, however. Certain dimensions of our self may become significantly disrupted by depression. Other dimensions may remain relatively free from significant disruption.

To use an analogy, a disease may alter the condition of my kidneys and as a result affect my heart rate. My heart, however, can remain healthy. It is affected but its basic core is not altered. I am a "sick" person but not all parts of me are contaminated.

That same dynamic may happen when we become depressed. We feel the effects of depression throughout our total self. Everything about us is touched by depression's power. But only certain dimensions of our self may become dysfunctional.

One way to determine the extent of our depression is to determine our level of self-disturbance. I have developed a chart showing the various levels of self-disturbance we might succumb to when we are depressed.

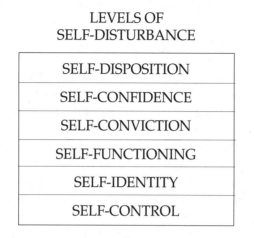

LEVELS OF
SELF-DISTURBANCE

| SELF-DISPOSITION |
| SELF-CONFIDENCE |
| SELF-CONVICTION |
| SELF-FUNCTIONING |
| SELF-IDENTITY |
| SELF-CONTROL |

Each descending level represents a more severe state of self-disturbance. Disturbance of self-disposition represents the least severe form. Disturbance of self-control represents the most severe form.

Each descending level incorporates those levels above it. A pastor suffering disturbance of self-confidence (second level) will also suffer disturbance of self-disposition (first level). A pastor suffering disturbance of self-conviction (third level) will typically experience disturbance of self-disposition (first level) and self-confidence (second level).

Each level does not incorporate those levels below it, however. Each level represents its own level of disturbance. For example, depression may primarily result in disturbance of a pastor's self-disposition. In this case the pastor's self-confidence, self-conviction, self-functioning, self-identity, and self-control will remain basically unaltered. The pastor's depression will affect these other aspects of the pastor's self but not cause significant damage to them. They remain re-sources of strength the pastor can rely upon.

Disturbed Self-disposition

The least severe form of fragmentation is disturbance of the pastor's disposition. The pastor's internal mood is altered. This level of self-disturbance is conveyed by the sentiment: *My work feels heavy.*

"I've lost my spark," said Reverend Merrill. "I once felt energetic about my work at the church, but lately I have a hollow feeling inside, a kind of heavy-heartedness. Each morning I try to pump myself up, but it hasn't helped. I can't get myself back in a decent mood."

Work at church had been stressful. "Certain parishioners are upset with the new programs I've started. They're not like the ones established by their beloved previous pastor who was there twenty-three years. As a result, attendance and giving are down, which causes further complaints among members. I've spent a good deal of time lately listening to people's concerns and trying to reassure them."

The criticisms bothered him—as well as the comparisons to the former pastor. Rather than deal with these feelings he pushed them aside. "The only solution, I've told myself, is to not pay attention to how I feel but simply to work harder." Deterioration of his body, mind, and spirit began to show, however.

A *vague sadness* arose within him, which gathered in old feelings of self-pity. Instead of going to work with a hopeful heart he went with a heavy chest. He felt *wiped out.* He wondered how he made it through Sunday mornings and committee meetings. His *desires diminished.* He had little interest in sex, for example, and little pleasure when it happened. He *ruminated.* He wondered if things at the church would ever be settled. He worried that maybe he would never feel excited about his work again. His *sleep pattern changed.* He would wake early in the morning and be unable to go back to sleep.

From the symptoms Reverend Merrill presented, we diagnosed that he was depressed. He was more than blue. He was depressed. But how depressed was he? What was his level of self-disturbance?

In telling his story, he made an observation that gave us a clue. "You know, in spite of my down mood I'm really not down on myself. I'm depressed by the responses of people, but I still think I'm doing a decent job. And I'm not ready to give up on them or on being a pastor. I know what God wants me to do. It's just that it's hard to get up the old enthusiasm, to feel energized. I'm not. I feel heavy and sad. That scares me, especially when it won't go away."

The dimension of his self disturbed by depression was his disposition. That was the basic extent of his fragmentation. While his depressed disposition colored all dimensions of his self, it did not significantly alter them. His self-confidence remained firm. Although at times frustrated with himself, he neither berated himself nor felt helpless. His self-conviction remained stable. The importance of his values, goals, and faith did not seriously wane, though he lacked the energy to fully enact or enjoy them. His self-functioning, self-identity, and self-control were basically intact. There were no appre-ciable declines in his work, in his sense of who he was, or in his management of himself.

Reverend Merrill was painfully depressed, but the degree of self-disturbance had reached only to the level of his self-disposition. Although I empathized with his struggle, I was grateful he was as healthy as he was.

Disturbed Self-confidence

The next level of severity is disturbed self-confidence. The pastor's inner assurance about himself or herself is shaken. This level of self-disturbance is conveyed by the sentiment: *I'm not sure I can do my work well.*

Reverend Fleming came for counseling after seven months of being the new minister at a rural church. At first she had been excited about the position. Now she felt despondent. The difficulty centered around persons in the church who were openly critical of her views and covertly critical of her being a female pastor—their first female pastor.

Reverend Fleming showed signs of being depressed. She had gained considerable weight in the last few months. She forgot things, lost things, and seemed in a daze. She felt helpless to change her situation. Tears flowed easily. Getting out of bed in the morning became increasingly difficult. Although she had not thought in detail about suicide, there were times when she imagined that it would be easier "not to be alive" than to go on as she was.

These were serious symptoms. What caused them? A recent medical exam showed no significant physical problems. She was not taking any medication that might have induced depression-like signs. After further assessment we decided that she was depressed. We made that our working diagnosis until we might find otherwise.

She did not seem depressed through and through, however. Besides her disposition, the dimension of her self most affected appeared to be her self-confidence. She had begun to seriously doubt herself. Criticism and lack of support had sapped her confidence in her own abilities. She wondered if she had what it takes to be a good minister.

I asked Reverend Fleming about the next level of self-disturbance, namely the level of self-conviction. "I understand that your enthusiasm has waned and your confidence has plummeted, but what about your convictions? Have serious doubts arisen within you about your faith? Do your values still seem important? Are you still inspired by people whose lives you've admired?"

She thought and then responded, "I doubt myself more than I doubt others. I've started to develop some negative thoughts about certain parishioners, but I'm not down on people in general or distrustful of them. I'm just less sure that I can get parishioners to respond to me as I want them to. I still think God cares about me, yet I don't always feel worthy of God. I still feel the value of the ideals I've brought into ministry, but I worry now that I won't be able to make them come alive in the church."

Reverend Fleming's depression had reached only the level of her self-confidence. She still retained strength in the area of self-conviction. Her self-functioning, self-identity, and self-control also remained firm. These would prove beneficial to her in the process of working through her depression.

Disturbed Self-conviction

More serious than disturbed self-disposition and self-confidence is disturbance of the pastor's self-conviction. The pastor's ideals begin to crumble. This level of self-disturbance is conveyed by the sentiment: *I'm no longer sure my work is worth doing.*

Reverend Kushner's wife had insisted he get counseling. She said he was depressed. He told her she didn't know what depression was. He did. He had seen it in others; he knew how bad it could be, and he wasn't there.

I asked him what it was his wife might have seen that would make her believe he was depressed. "Ordinary stuff," he replied. "After all these years, you find that all your assumed heroes have feet of clay. You come to realize there isn't anyone you can really count on, and not much you can rely on. You continue to do your work, but you wonder if it makes any real difference in people's lives. You go through the motions. You have to be tough and not let anything bother you. I suppose my wife sees the negative side of me coming out. I just call it being realistic."

If Reverend Kushner were depressed, as his wife suspected, his symptoms were not as obvious as in the cases of Reverend Merrill and Reverend Fleming. The symptoms of what he called his "realistic" side seemed to suggest a cynical person, not a depressed person. What was going on here?

I asked him when this "realistic" side of him had started to emerge. He then related a long history of disappointments and his responses to them. Gradually it became clear that Reverend Kushner's "realistic" attitudes were manifestations of a subtle, chronic depression. He had probably been depressed for a long time with mild to moderate symptoms that were, at times, hard to differentiate from his personality.

He lacked joyfulness. He was oversensitive to minor environmental frustrations. He tended to stifle pleasurable activities. He expressed futility. He subtly depreciated himself. These apparent personality traits were manifestations of his chronic depression. The stress of current disappointments threatened to turn his chronic depression into a major depression. The danger existed that he would fragment further. It was this potential disaster that his wife sensed.

At this point, however, his depression had reached only the level of his self-conviction. His realistic attitude expressed the erosion of hopes and ideals. Depressive cynicism stood in the place of sustaining convictions.

The slow forces of depression had more than altered Reverend Kushner's convictions. They had undermined his disposition and confidence. Overtly, however, his self-confidence did not seem altered. He seemed gruffly assured of his stance in life. I suspected otherwise. In most cases, a pastor's confidence is depleted before his or her convictions. In Reverend Kushner's case, it became clear that his gruff assurance was a cover and compensation for his depleted self-confidence.

In spite of his diminished values, ideals, and heroes, Reverend Kushner's capacities for self-functioning remained adequate. Although his work was often done mechanically, he still carried out his full slate of church duties.

His self-identity also remained intact. While his interpretation of who the minister should be became more rigid, he still had a firm hold on who he was and what he was called upon to do.

Finally, the self-control dimension of his self was preserved. Although he had become somewhat crusty with his wife, and occasionally with others outside the family, he was able to relate appropriately and regulate his behavior.

Reverend Kushner was in danger of becoming more severely fragmented. Fortunately he had retained firmness of self in several areas. These would form part of the bulwark against depression's advances.

Disturbed Self-functioning

An even more severe result of depression is disruption of a pastor's self-functioning. The pastor's capacity to carry out her or his duties deteriorates. This level of self-disturbance is conveyed by the sentiment: *I'm working less and less.*

Reverend Ortiz had been referred to counseling by her church consistory. "They say I'm letting things slip badly. Maybe I am. I can't tell whether there is just more work to do or if I'm not up to doing the work that was always there. I feel like giving up. But there's nothing I can do. The church council says that I have to find some help or else they will have to ask me to resign."

Reverend Ortiz had suffered depressive episodes in the past. She knew what the symptoms were. Her current ones were similar to previous ones. Before concluding that she was depressed again, however, we had her doctor run laboratory tests to check for such conditions as diabetes, thyroid problems, and estrogen deficiencies. Nothing significant was found. We suspected, then, that her symptoms were signs of a depressive disorder rather than a physiological illness.

The complaint from her congregation about her work suggested that her depression had reached at least the level of self-functioning. But was this just one of those typical complaints made by all frustrated churches?

The complaint was accurate. From asking Reverend Ortiz about her range of activities in the church, it became clear she had ceased to function adequately. She was failing not only to get the *right* things done but to get much of *anything* done. Calls were sporadically returned. Meetings were missed or attended late. Preparations for worship were haphazard. Routine administrative tasks were ignored. When asked how she spent her time, she said she visited shut-ins a lot.

Reverend Ortiz was withdrawing. Her depression had forced her into a secluded existence. As a result, she was failing to achieve the minimal level of efficiency which any church rightly expects. Her self-functioning capacity was severely compromised.

Compromised also were other dimensions of her self: her self-disposition, self-confidence, and self-conviction. The collapse of these dimensions had contributed to the collapse of her self-functioning. It was hard for her to do her work with her mood down, her confidence low, and her convictions gone.

Although it may seem meager, she fortunately retained her capacities for self-identity and self-control. She would need these, and support from others, to help her regain her self and maintain her job.

Disturbed Self-identity

An even more devastating level of depressive fragmentation is disturbed self-identity. The pastor's hold on personal reality becomes impaired. If conveyed at all, this level is represented by the sentiment: *I'm confused about who I am and what work I'm to do.*

Depression can stand pastors on their head. It can cause them to be not quite sure of who or where they are. Normal perceptions fade. Shadowy thoughts loom.

This level of self-disturbance is relatively uncommon. Pastors usually seek help or are forced to get it before they reach this state of deterioration. This state may also be short-lived. Pastors remain depressed but surface to higher levels of functioning as therapy and medication restore cohesion. And yet it does happen. At times an acute depressive reaction will send a pastor spiraling down to this level. When this happens, it is frightening to all.

Reverend Joberg was referred for counseling by a denominational leader. This leader had been contacted by Reverend Joberg's congregation. They were worried about him and somewhat afraid of him.

His behavior had changed. He no longer attended adequately to church duties. He no longer smiled or seemed cordial. No one seemed able to get through to him.

His thinking had changed. He expressed to certain parishioners that he felt watched and spied upon. "Some people in this church have it out for me," he said ominously. "They're working to get me fired." He believed that something bad was going to happen to his family. "Someone's going to get physically hurt, I just know it." He envisioned his family becoming destitute and having to go on welfare. He thought he probably had cancer or some other dreaded disease.

Reverend Joberg's surroundings seemed unreal to him. He felt strangely uncomfortable in familiar settings. He could no longer judge time or distances well. Nothing looked the way it used to.

Neither did he feel like himself. "My voice does not seem to belong to me. It's like something I hear rather than something that's coming from me." While externally he felt immobile, internally he felt sped up, as if he were running from place to place. He summed up his condition in these touching words: "My life has come apart in bits and pieces. I don't know what's happening from one day to the next, or really who I am from one day to the next."

Reverend Joberg's dreaded events had no apparent basis in reality. He was a beloved pastor. His family and their finances were stable. His physical health was sound. And yet here he was with paranoid thinking, delusional ideas, and symptoms of depersonalization.

Was Reverend Joberg in the midst of a psychotic break-down? It certainly looked like it. But after a series of physical and psychological assessments, it became apparent that he was not psychotic but rather severely depressed. Depression had resulted in a degeneration of his self-identity, of his personal hold on his sense of himself and reality. His paranoid thinking, delusional ideas, and depersonalized feelings were the disintegration products of his severe depression.

Strangely enough, that was good news. He did not need to be treated for psychosis. He was troubled by common depression, which would respond to treatment and eventually lift.

In spite of his debilitated state, he still maintained self-control. The last remnant of his cohesion had not been lost. He was ambulatory and communicative. At this level of depression, small blessings loom large.

Disturbed Self-control

The most severe level of depressive fragmentation is loss of self-control. The pastor's capacity for personal management is lost. If conveyed at all, this level is represented by the sentiment: *I am incapable of doing any work or doing anything.*

Depression can leave a pastor in a form the pastor and others scarcely recognize. The pastor's self is more than clouded. It is vacated. This condition, too, is rare. Prior to this level of self-disturbance, pastors usually seek help. If not, someone intervenes on their behalf. And yet, clergy do regress to this state. Pastors with prior bouts of depression, and pastors with other contributing emotional or biochemical problems, may succumb to this level of disintegration. Even single episodes of depression can lead to the collapse of any minister, no matter how firm the minister's self may have been.

The wife of Reverend Esling was upset. "I had to do it," she said, "although it was the most painful thing I have ever done." She had recently hospitalized her husband. He was getting worse and worse. There was nothing else she could do.

At first Reverend Esling was just extremely morose. "He'd walk around the house late at night, saying little, looking sad." He then began to stay home more and more, seldom going out, not even to church. Finally he had started to spend long periods in bed.

"He seemed to be in a stupor," Mrs. Esling said. "He'd move his arms and legs and head very little. When he did, it was in slow motion. He'd mumble one word responses if we could get him to respond at all." Personal care habits lapsed. "He stopped shaving and showering. He didn't clean himself well after going to the bathroom. He would nibble at food or just push it away when I tried to spoon-feed him. He started to look terrible."

Medical personnel ruled out physical problems such as a brain tumor or an insidious onset of Alzheimer's disease. Reverend Esling was severely depressed. Hospitalization was necessary to cope with the crisis. Mrs. Esling had come to find support for herself, and to find out how to help her husband through his difficult time.

Even in this depleted state there was hope. Pastors who have suffered this level of self-disturbance have recovered. They have regained healthy control, identity, functioning, convictions, confidence, and disposition. With the psalmist they have gratefully proclaimed, "He restoreth my soul" (KJV). Such testimonies sustain us at this darkest hour.

SUGGESTIONS FOR CAREGIVERS

Depressed pastors are subjects of talk. Much of that talk is concern rather than complaint. We family members and church parishioners truly want to help. Often we know not what to do. Almost always we lack a basis for whatever we *may* do. The idea of *levels of self-disturbance* can orient our work. It can help us determine a fitting *level of response.*

Understanding the levels of disturbance is easy. Identifying a particular pastor's level of disturbance may be difficult. Depression affects everything about the pastor's thinking and behaving. It may take time for us to determine a pastor's level of fragmentation. Keep trying. If you can't figure out what's altered, try to figure out what's *not* altered. Show the pastor the diagram on levels of self-disturbance and discuss together where the pastor might be. This contact itself is therapeutic.

What about levels of disturbance and suicide? A pastor at any level of disturbance may commit suicide. It is always a possibility. Family and lay caregivers, however, should not be judges. They should not be burdened with trying to determine how suicidal the pastor may be. Even professionals struggle with assessing the seriousness of suicidal threats.

What caregivers need to do *at every level of disturbance* is this:

1. Consider *every* insinuation, idea, or action regarding suicide as dangerous.
2. Regularly ask a depressed pastor about suicidal thoughts *and about suicide attempts.*
3. Share information about the pastor's suicide thoughts and attempts with appropriate others who can watch and be with the pastor.
4. Keep your guard up. Clergy, like other individuals, are often most at risk for suicide once the storm has passed. They have more energy then to do themselves harm.
5. Be prepared to intervene. Lovingly coerce the pastor to seek therapy, get medication, or be hospitalized.

Dealing directly with suicidal ideas and actions is always a fitting response. Furthermore, it's better to overdramatize the danger than to underplay it. Be a fool for love's sake.

The "Levels of Self-Disturbance" diagram helps us determine how fragmented the pastor has become. The following

"Levels of Response" diagram helps us determine how to give care best.

This "levels of response" approach has two aims. First, we caregivers do not want to intrude too much. Second, we do not want to intrude too little. We do not want to take over functions the depressed pastor is capable of doing and needs to do in order to work through depression. And yet we do not want to leave the pastor floundering in functions he or she is incapable of and thus more depressed by.

LEVELS OF RESPONSE TO SELF-DISTURBANCE

Levels of Disturbance	Levels of Response
SELF-DISPOSITION	EMPATHIZE
SELF-CONFIDENCE	AFFIRM
SELF-CONVICTION	DEMONSTRATE
SELF-FUNCTIONING	ASSIST
SELF-IDENTITY	CONTAIN
SELF-CONTROL	MANAGE

Each level of self-disturbance can be met with a specific response. For example, disturbed self-disposition is best met with the response of *empathy*. Disturbed self-confidence is best met with the response of *affirmation*.

A more severe level of disturbance can be approached also by the responses appropriate for less severe levels. The specific response for each level should remain central, however. Thus, a family aiding a pastor with disturbed self-conviction can respond with empathy and affirmation, but the central response should focus around *demonstration*.

Empathize for Disturbed Disposition

What does a pastor need when her or his mood is down? Since the pastor is functioning adequately in other areas, the pastor does not need advice or someone to take over. The pastor needs to feel understood. Self-disposition distur-bances call for caregivers to be empathic.

Being empathic is not being sympathetic. When we are sympathetic, we feel sorry for the pastor. We have compas-sion for him or her. There's nothing wrong with this. It's just not particularly helpful.

To be empathic, however, means to *feel with* the pastor. It is *standing by* the pastor; we sense what the pastor is going through and convey our understanding. As empathic caregivers, we refrain from saying, "I know how you feel." This sounds shallow. It also draws attention to us rather than to the pastor. Furthermore it is likely inaccurate. We do not really know how the pastor feels. Our experiences may be similar but not the same.

We can try, instead, to express what we sense about the pastor's feelings. We might say, for example: "This is a hard time for you. Your spirit seems heavy and troubled"; or "You probably worry that you'll never be your old self again"; or "At times you may feel that you can't go on anymore, don't even want to go on anymore."

Being empathic may mean sitting quietly with a pastor who does not feel like talking, putting our hand on the pastor's hand, or shaking our head in affirmation about how sad things seem to be. We resonate with the pastor's mood. We share it with him or her.

In this empathic role, we are not *giving reassurances*. We are being reassuringly present. We are not trying to pump up the pastor with declarations that everything will be all right. We are standing with the pastor by conveying our understanding.

This may be hard to do. Depression may be foreign to us. We don't understand what the pastor is suffering. Depression may be frightening to us. We're afraid to *feel with* the pastor lest we, too, become depressed. Depression may anger us. We're not inclined to coddle the pastor with understanding.

Empathic understanding, however, is often all the pastor needs. Empathy conveys to the pastor that he or she is not alone. Others not only care but are in touch. That assurance alone has healing power.

Being empathic is important at every level of self-disturbance. It is the basic response underlying all recovery from depression. It supports other responses which must become central when fragmentation increases. But when only a pastor's mood is disturbed, our empathic responses alone are fitting and sufficient.

Affirm for Disturbed Confidence

When a pastor's self-confidence begins to slip, we caretakers can be affirming. While still empathic, we focus on affirming the pastor's abilities and goodness. We might say, for example: "You are better than you think you are, and you can do more than you think you can"; or "Although you may not see it, your sermons still touch people's hearts"; or "You've lost your confidence but not your abilities"; or "I doubt God sees you as negatively as you see yourself."

Affirmations must be authentic. Exaggerated compliments are patronizing. Depressed pastors are sensitive to this phoniness. They feel belittled rather than appreciated. Affirmation must also be regulated. Excessive compliments are overwhelming. Depressed pastors cannot absorb them. They feel obligated to affirm the efforts of the affirmer.

Our affirmation can be supported by interpretations. We can gently interpret to the pastor why his or her self-esteem has been eroded. We might say: "When depression hits, one's self-esteem is usually the first casualty"; or "Depression tries to convince us that all the good we believed about our self is shamefully false."

Going beyond affirmation at this point may undermine the very confidence we are trying to uphold. Self-esteem is jeopardized further when we give advice to the pastor who is still capable of making decisions or when we suggest taking over certain duties the pastor is still capable of handling. Our fitting responses should be directed to the pastor's level of disturbance, not the pastor's levels of strength.

Demonstrate for Disturbed Conviction

Disturbances of self-conviction call for caregivers to be *demonstrative*. We focus on displaying the presence and power of certain values. This can be done in several ways.

First, we *hold up* those convictions which have been central to the pastor. Depressed pastors tend to forget. We remind them. We demonstrate the power of certain values in the lives of people the pastor knows. We reveal the meaningfulness of beliefs for churches the pastor has loved. We point to faithfulness in the pastor which both represents health and preserves well-being. We express convictions through prayer, and ask God to restore power in the pastor's life.

Second, we *hold on* to convictions for the pastor until he or she is able to reclaim them. We might say, "I know these values and beliefs do not mean very much to you right now, but I'll hold on to them for you and treasure them until you're able to make them your own again." We become custodians of convictions. We keep safe for the pastor those ideals the pastor is incapable of protecting. This reassures and liberates. It allows the pastor to stop worrying so much about losing a part of the self while struggling to find a way through depression.

Finally, we *hold to* those convictions. We demonstrate them in our own living. Depressed pastors are easily disillu-sioned. Our behavior should be no cause for further grief. We serve as God's agents of healing when we demonstrate integrity.

Our demonstrations can be supported by suggestions. We may suggest, for example, that the pastor continue *to act the part*. Even though certain things feel empty, the pastor can act as if they did not. *Acting the Christian's part*, for instance, is advantageous. It keeps the pastor functioning in faithful ways. It induces the return of the very feelings which presently are gone.

We may also suggest that the pastor not act on present feelings. This is not the time to make major decisions. One's perspective is skewed. It is not to be trusted.

We must avoid being preachy, however. We must refrain from overwhelming with logic. We are not attempting to *infuse* convictions. We are attempting to *lift up* convictions. We keep alive a reality that has temporarily disappeared for the pastor.

Assist for Disturbed Functioning

Self-functioning disturbances call for caregivers to *assist*. Because the pastor is floundering in his or her duties, we need to participate with the pastor.

We assist by becoming an *auxiliary ego*. Pastors with self-functioning disturbances have not totally stopped doing. In their depleted state, however, capacities for organization have been compromised. They do not prioritize. They attend to easy tasks rather than difficult tasks. To avoid pressure, they respond to "squeaky wheel" demands no matter how superficial. Their attention span dwindles down to the next moment rather than the next day.

We assist the pastor by helping structure life. We become an assistant to the pastor's ego, to the pastor's organizing capacities. A spouse, for example, might help the depressed pastor write up a list of priorities for the next day. The spouse might remind the pastor the following morning of the plan they've made: "So, you're going to look at your list before beginning your day, right? And you'll start with the first task listed and go on down, checking them off when completed?"

Parishioners can also serve as auxiliary egos. They may remind the pastor of important dates. They may aid the pastor in making and following agendas. They may help the pastor put boundaries on inappropriate requests.

We caregivers can also become *auxiliary hands*. We literally help with tasks. A spouse might assist by making phone calls, setting up appointments, or helping the pastor with a program. Parishioners may help by sharing more of the Sunday service, shouldering more responsibility for new members, or making special arrangements.

Depressed pastors at this level often want others to take over. We caregivers should avoid the temptation. Our aim is to enable the pastor, not to enable the depression. We assist the pastor primarily to keep him or her moving. Keeping functional, even minimally, is healthy. One step in front of another keeps the self of the pastor active and wards off further encroachment of depression.

Contain for Disturbed Identity

Self-identity disturbances call for caregivers to *contain*. The pastor's personal hold on reality has slipped. We try to contain further erosion of the pastor's identity. Several approaches are necessary, although admittedly difficult.

First, *we contain others' reactions*. People talk. They talk about the depressed pastor. They often draw wrong conclusions. Their attitudes toward the pastor may change. The pastor's public identity may be devalued. We can try to preserve the pastor's reputation by trying to contain the negative reactions of family and parish members.

We do this by giving explanations. We might say: "She's struggling with depression right now. That's the reason for the strange symptoms. But it's a temporary condition. With time and understanding she'll be her old self again." We also ask others to greet the pastor with the respect and affection they've always had. We urge them to keep the pastor in their prayers. We implore them to speak well about the pastor to others.

Second, *we contain acting-out.* Depression shows. The weakened pastor shows it more. Little effort is made to curb displays of depressed feelings. This can damage the pastor's public identity. It can also damage the pastor's own personal integrity. Pastors often feel mortified by actions they've done when depressed. We can try to preserve the pastor's integrity by trying to contain the pastor's acting-out.

A direct approach is required. It does not help to say to the pastor, "Keep things in perspective." The pastor at this level has lost much of that capacity. All experiences tend to be equally driven by depression. There is no depression-free zone in which the pastor may stand to get perspective.

Therefore we give directions, if not commands. We might say: "When you go to the meeting, don't talk about feeling strange or about thinking that people have it in for you"; or "Make sure that you say hello to everyone. If you can smile, that's fine, but at least be civil"; or "Don't start asking people what other people have been saying about you." This is not patronizing. It's preserving.

Third, *we contain self-image.* Memories fade. A pastor's hold on private identity weakens. We can try to preserve the pastor's sense of self by trying to contain his or her self-images. We do this by fostering a sense of continuity in the pastor. A pastor in this state loses a sense of being the same person from day to day, from place to place. Therefore, in the presence of the pastor we may rehearse the history of who the pastor has been. We may remind the pastor of who he or she is now. We may reflect on hopes for what the pastor can become.

In severe cases of identity confusion, we show the pastor pictures, awards, and letters that cite the pastor's identity. We surround the pastor with familiar objects that stimulate a hold on personal reality. We ask the pastor to pray, read scripture aloud, and join in the singing of hymns as ways of enacting her or his self-image and thus keeping it viable.

Manage for Disturbed Control

Self-control disturbances call for caregivers to *manage*. Pastors have lost the ability to maintain themselves. We must take over. We caregivers now become caretakers. We become a substitute for the pastor's own self. We feed, dress, and take the pastor to the bathroom. We handle all the family's business matters. We inform the church of the pastor's present inability to lead. We take control of all medical decisions and treatment plans, including hospitalization.

This is an awesome responsibility. It frightens us. Deciding on hospitalization or electroconvulsive therapy (ECT) is difficult, for example. We feel incompetent to make such decisions. But if faced with the necessity, we cannot turn away.

Through it all we can be sustained by this thought: we manage only temporarily. We manage in order to preserve the pastor's capacity for self-management. We take control now so that the pastor can resume control later.

Suggestions for Clergy

Ask for help. More than that, ask for special help. Ask the hand that has been offered to change its grip so that you can grasp it better. If possible, share the "Levels of Response" diagram with others. Let them know what's helpful and what's not.

Do this even if you don't feel like it.
Do this even if you think you're not worth it.
Do this even if you doubt others really care.
Do this even if you're doing little else.
Do this even if you're confused.

Do this even though there's not much else you can do.

CHAPTER THREE

Causes of Our Depression

Depression melts the mind. It leaves us listless and unmotivated, with reduced capacities to concentrate. Depressed clergy, like others, look for easy explanations. They seek quick answers in the hope of feeling well again. Reflection is difficult.

Reflection, however, is indispensable. Discovering causes gives direction for cure. Searching for the roots of our depression sets us on the path to recovery. Our depression, furthermore, warrants an explanation beyond some general idea of the human condition. Our struggles deserve particular attention because each one of us is a special child of God whose depression is uniquely our own.

We depressed clergy understand this. Even though not fully functional, we tend to cooperate to the best of our ability. The remnant of health inside us joins in the work to overcome our depression.

CLAIMS FOR SINGLE CAUSES

A pastor's depression is multi-determined. That means it has several causes. This is becoming a common understanding in mental health circles. Less and less is depression said to be caused by a single factor. Such claims are still made, however.

Some declare that depression is caused by chemical imbalances in the brain. Depression, therefore, is considered a physical disease rather than a mental illness. Medication should be the primary mode of treatment. Only biological psychiatrists, consequently, are said to be qualified to deal with depression because only they understand how medications affect brain chemistry.

What's right about this claim? First, the implication that depression is not the result of a defect in character. Second, the implication that depression does involve some type of biophysical factor.

What's wrong with this claim? First, the reduction of depression to just a simple flaw in chemistry. Second, the minimizing of stressful situations and particular meanings a person gives to life as causes of depression. I personally have never treated a case of depression over an extended period of time that seemed to be caused solely by a biochemical imbalance.

Others claim that depression is caused by defective thinking. Persons become depressed because of misinterpretations, faulty processing of information, or negative thinking about self, experiences, or the future. Depression, therefore, is not considered an *affective* (emotional) disorder but a *cognitive* (thinking) disorder. Although recognizing that several factors play into depression, this model asserts that cognitive difficulties are central.

This claim is right in lifting up the role of a person's thoughts in causing depression. It is wrong in suggesting that depression is more a flaw in thinking than anything else. Environmental and biophysical factors are not sufficiently acknowledged.

Others maintain that depression is caused by stressful life events. Persons may become depressed through the death of a loved one, divorce, being fired from work, personal injury, or social rejection. Stressful events are considered the cardinal sources of depression. Biophysical reactions and disturbed thinking are seen as consequences rather than causes of depression.

This claim is right in accenting the impact of stressful events upon our mood. It is wrong in suggesting that events themselves have this power regardless of what meaning we give to them or how our body reacts to them.

THE DEPRESSION TRIANGLE

From my research and clinical experience, it appears that causes for depression fall into three interrelated categories. We can call this "the depression triangle." Pastors and I use this triangle to help determine the specific causes of their depression.

The Depression Triangle

Situation

Meaning   Body

A pastor's depression arises through the interaction of *situations* impinging on the pastor, *meanings* the pastor lives by, and *body processes* within the pastor. This interplay between environmental factors, cognitive factors, and biophysical factors is responsible for depression.

When a pastor's spouse dies, for example, the pastor may become depressed. This depression is fueled by the triangle of situation, meaning, and body. There is a *situation,* namely the death of the spouse. There is the *meaning* the pastor gives to this situation. There is a *body* reaction to this situation. Every depressive episode is caused by some mixture of situation, meaning, and body.

Any of these three may be a leading cause. Or they may essentially work in equal measure to generate a depressive reaction. For example, one pastor was hit hard by the death of her husband. They had shared forty years of marriage and ministry. Without children, she was now alone. This was the situation she was facing.

"He was all I had," she wept. "I was only complete as long as he was with me. Now there is nothing for me. I've died too. I might as well be down there in the grave with him." This was the type of meaning she gave to the situation.

She began to experience headaches and pain in her joints. Refusing to eat, and sleeping little, she became weak and constipated. This confirmed her feeling of being dead inside. These physical discomforts, along with her interpretation that life was over for her, led her to withdraw—and thus to be and to feel more alone. This in turn led to further rumina- tions and physical symptoms. These were the contributions of her body to the situation.

What caused this pastor's depression? Was it the highly stressful situation of losing her spouse, the most disturbing life event of all according to many rating scales? Was it her mental orientation that caused her to picture herself as in- complete and helpless unless he were there to make her whole? Or was it her physiological reactions that magnified her stress, confirmed her negative meanings, and eroded her energy for recovery? Asked another way, did her depression start with the death of her husband, with her tendency to see herself as helpless, or with her inclination to react to stressful events with body-depleting responses?

All three were involved. All were leading causes. This pastor needed help with every part of the depression trian- gle. Where to begin, and where to put the greatest emphasis, would be determined by her and her counselor.

Frequently there are several leading causes from each part of the depression triangle. One minister's wife was divorcing him at the same time that his church was enraged about policies he had initiated. These were the situations promot- ing depression in him. He habitually looked at things in a negative light, frequently saw himself as a victim, and doubted whether God really cared about him. These were the meanings supporting his depression. He was struggling with alcoholism and came from a family with a history of depression. These were the conditions of his body fostering depression.

Other times there is clearly just one leading cause. That cause either predisposes a pastor to depression or precipitates the depression. What role do the other parts of the depression triangle play in these cases? They function as *contributing causes.* They either push the pastor over the edge if the pastor is on the brink of depression, or they keep the depression going if the depression has already started.

For example, the leading cause of one pastor's depression was a chronic tendency to view himself in a negative light. He saw himself as weak and helpless. He believed that the bad things that happened to him were somehow his fault. He was inclined to interpret the actions of others as critical or rejecting. He was certain God was ready to swat him down for being a sinner. These particular ways of giving meaning to his self, experiences, and future predisposed him to become depressed.

That predisposition became a reality. Two contributing causes moved this pastor to a state of clinical depression. One was the news that for the third straight year the church council had decided not to raise his salary. This was the contributing situation. He took this negative news, a blow in itself, as confirmation of his negative view of himself.

Furthermore, in the midst of this stress, his chronic colitis flared up severely, curtailing his work and convincing him even more of his weakness and vulnerability. This body factor was the second contributing cause.

The convergence of these leading and contributing causes induced a state of depression in him. While all parts of the triangle needed aid, the meaning dimension would eventually require the greatest attention.

MULTIPLYING EFFECTS

In depression, the total effect is greater than the sum of the individual effects. The stress of a situation is not added to the stress of a meaning, to which is added the stress of a body factor. One bad, plus one bad, plus one bad does not equal three times the bad. It equals *many times* the bad.

That's because situation, meaning, and body affect one another and, in turn, are affected by the effect they have had on the others. Each cause multiplies the power of the others and then is multiplied by the power it has helped multiply in the others. We saw this happen in the pastor who lost her husband.

This insight helps us understand the tremendous power of causes in depression. Even apparently minor or passing events can magnify each other's power to the point of bringing about depression.

Furthermore, depression, like a fire, creates its own momentum. The hotter the depression the more it generates *its own* destructive situations, meanings, and bodily reactions. If this is not stopped, a pastor may reach a state of total collapse. This is why early intervention is so important. Defusing the escalating power of causes preserves what strength the pastor still possesses.

SPECIFIC FACTORS

Various situations may spur depression. Many are commonly acknowledged as traumatic events: death of a loved one, loss of a job, divorce, serious illness, and physical and sexual assaults, for example. Others are acknowledged as stressful circumstances: financial struggles, family problems, absence of social support, physical disabilities, unfulfilled dreams, and cultural restrictions.

Situations unique to an individual may nurture depression: the pastor is not selected for a church position, or is criticized by the church council, or sees church attendance and giving decline sharply, or has a book of sermons rejected for publication. To the world these may not seem like big deals, but to the pastor they may be.

Within the depression triangle, the *most common* leading cause is a recent stressful event. That event may be a major event in itself or it may be a final straw event. Stressful situations can accumulate, piled one on top of another, so that a final, apparently minor, event can unleash the power of all the preceding events.

Meanings involved in depression include all those thoughts, feelings, beliefs, attitudes, and wishes that lead a person to interpret life in unhelpful ways. Some of those meanings arise from faulty processing of information. For example, a pastor may misread, overgeneralize, draw illogical inferences, or personalize (relate external events to the pastor's self when there is no basis for making such a connection).

Other negative meanings spring from habitual ways of interpreting life. Certain assumptions undermine the pastor, such as the thought, "I have to do everything perfectly, or I'm a failure." Narrow religious beliefs may lead the pastor to distort experiences or to miss God's grace in them. Negative thoughts about self, relationships, and the future encourage low self-esteem, isolation, and hopelessness. Tendencies to depreciate events or to consider even small ones catastrophic inhibit the pastor from facing life realistically and wholesomely. Still other debilitating meanings occur through cognitive defects: immature, simplistic thinking; paranoid and delusional thoughts; and mental deficiencies linked with retardation, strokes, or senility.

Within the depression triangle, the leading cause *most resistant* to change is a person's network of meanings. They become inscribed on the mind and heart. Relinquishing them, even if they are damaging, is experienced as losing part of one's customary self.

Body factors that might contribute to depression include all dimensions of our biophysical self. Chemical imbalances affecting neurotransmitters in the brain induce depression. Genetic factors influence the risk of depression, in part by altering the individual's sensitivity to stressful life events. Diseases may include depression as part of their symptom picture, such as in Parkinson's disease, multiple sclerosis, and the onset of cancer. Medications and other chemical substances, such as alcohol, can cause depression. Chronic body weakness, hypochondriasis, and somatic inclinations (the tendency to live out stressful situations through one's body) may also contribute to depression in certain individuals.

Within the depression triangle, the *most insidious* leading cause is a biophysical condition. This factor is not easily detected. Often it must be inferred. As a result, the body's role in depression may be minimized. Conversely, body processes may be elevated as the most important, if not sole, cause of depressive episodes.

Recommendations for Clergy
1. Draw a triangle. Write "Situations" at one corner, "Meanings" at another, and "Body" at the third. Let this diagram guide your thoughts as you and those helping you look for causes.
2. Review situations. Think back to the last time you felt good on a regular basis. Use this as a way of detecting what situation(s) may have precipitated your depression. Don't always look for big events. Depression can start with apparently small incidents. Write down those situations on your diagram.
3. Investigate your meanings. Look for negative, automatic, or distorted thoughts. Ask someone you trust to assess the quality of your thinking and reasoning.

Write down possible meanings that may contribute to your depression.

4. Check your body. Familiarize yourself with the history of depression and major diseases in your family. Consult with a physician if you have gone without a medical exam for a while or if your depression persists after counseling and medication. Scrutinize your eating, drinking, and medication habits. Reflect on how you physically react to stressful situations. Write down those body factors that may participate in your depression.

5. Hypothesize about causes. Surmise which may be leading causes and which may be contributing causes. Draw arrows between parts of the triangle to indicate how each might have particularly affected the others. Modify your depression triangle as situation, meaning, and body become clearer.

6. Take all the data you have gathered and shape it into a personalized statement about your depression. Make that statement as heartfelt and accurate as you can.

CHAPTER FOUR

Our Renewal Tasks

How will *your* depression lift?

C. Welton Gaddy writes that his recovery started when he found a more honest community in the hospital than he had ever known in church.[1] William Hulme states that his recovery began after he received ECT treatments.[2] Thomas Moore describes how a priest's recovery came through allowing depression to have a central place in his life.[3] Other pastors indicate that their depression eased as they became engaged in a creative process, such as writing or painting. Still others say their depression just disappeared.

God's Spirit heals in many ways. How that Spirit lifts your depression will be unique to you. And yet, your experience will likely share similarities with those of other pastors. Recovery stories have much in common. The specific healing *event* may be different, but the underlying recovery *process* seems the same.

Somewhere along the line, our depression stops its down-ward spiral. We get as bad as we're going to get. We stay at that stopping place for a while, catching our breath. We then start to return to our old self. We recover. Then, if we're fortunate, we move beyond our old self and become even stronger than we were before we became depressed.

This recovery process is not unique to depression. We implicitly recognize that all recovery involves stabilization, convalescence, rejuvenation, and transformation. Ill persons stabilize (stop becoming worse), convalesce (gather energies), rejuvenate (return to normal), and hopefully become transformed (build up immunities to the illness).

These obvious steps in the process of healing also underlie our recovery from depression. As noted in our introduction, we will call these steps *applying brakes, holding still, returning home, and stepping beyond.*

This recovery process is seldom smooth. Often there is the familiar "two steps forward, one step back" movement. We may start to return to our old self, for example, but then regress. Our depression may become as bad as it ever was— or worse. The process then has to start over.

We might also become stuck in one step of the process. A pastor's struggle with depression may be dominated by the effort to keep it in check, for example. Not getting worse absorbs all the pastor's time and energy. Long periods may be spent by another pastor in holding still. The pastor does not get worse but does not get better either. Frequently the return to one's old self dominates the process. Rejuvenation comes in slow inches rather than swift strides. Deriving a blessing from depression may be the most difficult step. The episode of depression may pass without leaving the pastor newfound strength.

AIDING THE PROCESS

Pastors and I *join* this recovery process. We rely upon its movement. We follow its lead. We use it as a guide. Most important, pastors and I also try to *aid* this recovery process. We work intentionally to implement its progress. While the recovery process occurs naturally (depression, remember, will likely lift of its own accord in due time), we consider each recovery step as presenting us with a renewal task.

We try to aid stabilization by *applying brakes.* We try to aid convalescence by *holding still.* We try to aid rejuvenation by *returning home.* And we try to aid transformation by *stepping beyond.*

Renewal tasks are dictated by where the pastor is in the recovery process. For example, pastors are not in a position to try to return home while their depression is getting worse. They first need to apply brakes and then to hold still. Nor are pastors in a position to try to step beyond when they have yet to return home. There is an order to recovery. It is better to join and aid that process than to bypass it.

Unfortunately, we pastors often attempt activities for which we are not ready. As a result, we make matters worse for ourselves. For example, one pastor became frustrated when his elaborate efforts at meditation failed to deepen his spirituality and lessen his depression. Consequently, he felt even more spiritually inadequate, and his self-confidence was further eroded. He also began to feel abandoned by God as his self-convictions were shaken. The problem was not in meditation as a means of healing. Nor was it in the sincerity of the pastor. The problem was in his timing. His still expand-ing depression made it improbable that he would benefit significantly from meditation. He needed simpler spiritual exercises directed at applying brakes and holding on. Elabo-rate meditative efforts would more likely prove beneficial in the returning home and stepping beyond phases.

Applying Brakes

O God, don't clobber me in disgust
or chastise me in anger.
But the fact is, I'm falling apart.
I am distraught and confused
I am in deep trouble,
and I don't know how long I can take it.
(Psalm 6)[4]

We can recognize ourselves in this and other psalms re-written by Leslie Brandt. We know how our depression fragments us. We worry about where it's going to end and what will happen to us.

Our task at this stage is to apply brakes. We have to stop our depression from getting us into deeper trouble. To do that, we first define our depression triangle. We determine what situations, meanings, and body factors are fueling our depression. Then, through our own resources and the help of others, we decide how to respond to those situations, meanings, and body factors in order to stop their expanding impact on us.

We yearn, of course, for positive life changes. We pray for something good to happen to us to lift our spirits. We can't control the appearance of positive life changes, however. They come when they will.

What we can do is work to remove the difficulties that make us depressed. At this stage we best pray not so much for something good to happen as for the wisdom and strength to tackle our problems.

Applying brakes, therefore, basically entails difficulty re-moval. We try to remove the difficulties that particular situ-ations, meanings, and body factors create for us.

HOLDING STILL

God spoke to me today,
breaking through my childish doubts
with words of comfort and assurance.
    "Hang in there; sit tight;
stick to My course for your life," God said,
    "I will not let you down."

(*Psalm 110*)[5]

After being drained by depression, and after the exertion of applying brakes, we need to rest. We need to sit tight, to convalesce, before the long journey of returning home.

Depression, however, makes us impatient. We want to get better right away. Often, therefore, we ignore this period of holding still. We come out of the hospital too soon. We cut back on our medication or therapy too soon. We take up responsibilities too soon. Family members and parishioners frequently recognize that our efforts are pre-mature. We, however, may revert to denial, claiming we feel fine.

We need a period of holding still. We also need to enhance it. To do that, we try to determine how to respond to situations, meanings, and body factors so that we might regain our strength.

RETURNING HOME

Revive my flagging spirit, O God.
Restore to me the joy and assurance
  of a right relationship with You.
Reinstate me in Your purposes,
  and help me to avoid
    the snares and pitfalls along this earthly path.
                          (Psalm 51) [6]

In a larger sense, returning home extends from our first effort to apply brakes to our final effort to step beyond. Stated spiritually, returning home begins with facing what we've become and ends by living what God would have us be.

At the same time, returning home is also a specific phase of recovery. Although the lines blur between a period of convalescence (holding still) and rejuvenation (returning home), we implicitly know when we are on the mend. We are vulnerable to relapses at this time, however. There are snares and pitfalls along the way. Yet we rejoice that our self is returning to normal.

We can aid this journey. We can deal with situations, meanings, and body factors in ways that move us along the path. This may or may not hasten our journey. It does, however, keep us traveling in the right direction and on the right road.

STEPPING BEYOND

God is in our midst,
aware of the fears and apprehensions
of us beloved children.
God may not always rid us of our fears,
but God does promise to face them with us,
to make them stepping-stones of faith,
to use them to draw us closer
to God's very self.

(Psalm 11)[7]

Depression is more than a condition. It is a great question. It forces us to look at the quality of our life and at its foundations. Overcoming depression can be more than recovery. It can be transformation. Through God's grace our depression becomes a birth canal for new life.

Part of our task is to assist in this creating. Dealing with our depression includes the task of stepping beyond. We try to wrestle a blessing from our depression. We look deep within the situations, meanings, and body factors of our depression for signals of grace that may transform us.

ENCOURAGEMENT FOR THE PROCESS

These renewal tasks are difficult, but we cannot avoid them. No matter what our level of self-disturbance, we must actively participate in our own recovery. That may be minimal at times. We may barely be able to get up from bed, for example. But each small act toward our own good is curative. Just *hanging in there* favors the healing process.

During all this we will need to lean upon others. We cannot go it alone. But the help we seek should be assistance for helping ourselves. Restoration of our self, not relinquishing our self, is our aim. No help, therefore, is too embarrassing or too belittling if it serves the purpose of renewing our soul.

For our soul *is* involved in these renewal tasks. The very core of our personhood is at stake. Our unique identity, our capacity to love passionately, our sensitivity to God's grace-filled gestures—all these and more are the gifts we strive to save.

Although spiritually weakened by depression, let us imbue each act and occasion with holy significance. Feebly, but persistently, let us imagine every moment as throbbing with God's renewing power, and from this vacillating aura of hope, let us ask for wisdom, seek divine strength, and give thanks for every opportunity to reclaim our life.

CHAPTER FIVE
Applying Brakes

Dear God, keep each of us pastors from being our own worst enemy. Help us use the opportunities you provide to avoid the hazards that can lead us deeper into depression. Amen.

Halt downward sliding. That's our first renewal task. Here we do not reflect on what we should have done to keep from being depressed. We focus, instead, on what we need to do to keep from getting worse. The following discussion does not cover all circumstances in which applying brakes is necessary. Nor are the offered suggestions the only ways to apply brakes. This chapter simply identifies typical skids that endanger us pastors and basic ways to resist.

Guidelines for applying brakes:
1. Determine the leading cause(s) of your depression. As you start, work on no more than a total of two suggestions for applying brakes. Pick those suggestions which most pertain to you. Work on other ways of applying brakes after you have sufficiently accomplished the first ones.
2. Stay with the renewal task of applying brakes until you have emotionally stabilized. Determine when you have

stabilized by your own assessment and the assessment of those helping you. Braking will likely take longer than you think. Don't rush.

3. Even as you eventually work on other renewal tasks, periodically assess how well you are keeping depression in check. Applying brakes is a continuous process, easier later but always necessary.

SITUATIONS

Difficult times foster depressed feelings. We know that personally. Clinical studies concur. The good news is that as stressful situations diminish, our depression also diminishes. The bad news is that as stressful situations expand, our depression also expands. Our first task is to avoid the bad news.

We do that by dealing with a primary cause of depression's spread: approaches to difficult situations that make them worse. At the applying brakes stage, we focus not on solving situations but on halting our unhealthy reactions to them.

Does this mean we let situations go on? Are we to spend all our time attempting to curb our unhealthy reactions rather than handling the situations causing us pain? Situations causing depression do need correction—but not here. Our first renewal task is to get our self in hand. Our depressive situations have usually been there for a while. They have not suddenly appeared, although for us they may suddenly seem like a crisis. Our aim can be this: to carry out our responsibilities at home and work as best we can while attempting to correct our debilitating responses to depressive situations. This act itself can go a long way toward resolving our situational difficulties.

Stop Avoidant, Repetitive, or Fixing Approaches

1. Halt avoidance. Cease turning your head away. "I'm going to ignore the problem," said one minister injured by church dissension. "I'll just act like it isn't there." This was not a healthy act of benign neglect in a situation that required healing space. It was wholesale withdrawal. The pastor achieved momentary relief but the problem remained. Worse than that, if left unattended, the problem could breed new dissension compounding the pastor's stress.

Although we may not know specifically *what* to do in certain situations, we are doing *something* when we put brakes on our avoidance. The Scriptures encourage us to take heart, not to take cover. Facing a problem, even if we just stand there, is the first step in solving it. Facing a problem, rather than avoiding it, is the first step in curbing our depression.

2. Halt repetitive acts. Refrain from chronic patterns of response. One depressed pastor lapsed into automatic apology and appeasement when confronted with difficulty. This was not a healthy act of contrite adjustment in a situation that required ownership of responsibility. It was mechanical behavior. While it brought momentary soothing to the pastor, it furthered his depression. Difficult situations remained and festered. Support diminished as people perceived his action as ineffective and him as insincere.

Although we may be fearful of giving up our routines, halting repetitive acts limits depression's spread. It also allows our energy to be used more productively.

3. Halt trying to fix. Suspend disconnected efforts to make situations go away. In an effort to ease our stressful situations, we may anxiously attempt this, then that, then the next thing. This is not a healthy act of faithful searching in situations that require special consideration. It is frantic scrambling. We are too reactive to be responsive.

Reverend Fleming, whom we met in chapter 2, lamented her ability to handle parishioners who were upset with her views and gender. She was bright. Her intentions were good. But we began to see that she lacked a strategy for resolving these issues. Instead, she made disconnected stabs at fixing them.

She would ignore comments, try to please, or appeal for justice from the pulpit. She would keep quiet in groups or attempt to micromanage them. She would attempt to impress: "Surely when the people see how dedicated I am, how loving I've been, or how exhausted I've become, surely, surely the situation will change." She would attempt to beseech: She immersed herself in long meditation and prayer that she hoped would move God to rescue her from her plight.

For Reverend Fleming, as for most of us, her fixing was erosive. Because she lacked a consistent strategy for resolving her problems, they persisted and toxified. Furthermore, certain acts were socially and pastorally inappropriate, and these caused their own unique damage. In addition, the congregation increasingly interpreted her efforts as signs that she lacked confidence and know-how. This further undercut her pastoral credibility.

Perhaps the most serious effect of her fixing was the drain on her spirit. The more her fixing stabs failed, the more she felt ineffective, panicky, and helpless. As a result, she tried even more desperately to fix, which again inflamed her situation, which again in turn deepened her depression. Although trying to fix was a sign that she had not given up, it unfortunately pulled her closer to that abyss.

Applying brakes to our fixing efforts is a positive step in our own renewal. When I suggested to Reverend Fleming that she stop trying to fix things, she sat stunned. Slowly a tight smile formed to hold back tears, and a deep weariness in her eyes gave way to a look of grateful relief. "I've sensed that none of this was helping, that in fact it was probably making me more miserable. But I was afraid to stop. I thought it would mean I was giving up, that I was helpless. But it doesn't have to mean that. It can just mean that I won't try so hard to make things better that I make situations and my depression worse." Such an understanding was a blessing to her. It can be for many of us.

Stop Non-Talk or Lax Talk

1. End silence. Quit being mum about depressive situations. Bottling problems preserves them while souring the mixture. We saw this happen initially with Reverend Merrill in chapter 2. Rather than communicate about the situations causing him stress, he simply buttoned his lip, lowered his head, and worked harder. As a result the heaviness inside intensified.

Not talking is not a sign of being a strong silent type. Nor is it a sign of sparing others. Not talking is usually a sign of grandiosity or helplessness. In both cases the message is: *Nobody can help me.*

Talk about what you're facing. Talk regularly, for a significant stretch of time. Find a person or group to listen who is available, healthy, and empathic. Formally or informally contract with them for times to talk about your depressive situations.

Talking is not a cure-all, but there is no cure at all without talking. In general, talking helps get things off our chest. It clarifies what's really troubling us. It reassures us that someone cares. In these ways talking becomes a means of applying brakes to situations depressing us.

2. End lax talk. Monitor what comes out of your mouth. Resist indiscriminate talk. Abstain from talking to everyone or anyone about your problems. Guard against unburdening yourself in sermons, pastoral calls, and council meetings. Beware of overtaxing your spouse with your complaints and worries.

Resist narrow-feeling talk. Rather than expressing only certain feelings you have about situations, express all the feelings you have about them. Convey not only helpless or angry feelings, for example, but also ambivalent feelings, wishful feelings, positive feelings, and feelings too deep for words.

Why? Because situations impinging upon us need to stay supple. When we're depressed, we feel empty and flat, and we speak in ways that are empty and flat. If we continue, we begin to perceive the world around us, including our stress-ful situations, as being as empty and flat as our feelings and words. A gray-felt world becomes a gray-spoken world and then a gray-perceived world.

Life is richer than that. Even depressive situations have more emotional vitality to them than we grasp—or even want to admit. Narrow-feeling talk crystallizes difficult situations. Expressing wider ranges of feelings keeps us and situations supple.

Also resist personalized talk. We backslide if we merely personalize depressing situations rather than also external-izing them. In personalizing we respond to situations in terms of their private meaning and impact on us. Depressing situations are lived as events happening *to me* rather than also as events *to be resolved*. One depressed pastor recognized the danger: "I'm so inclined to look at everything that happens in the church as somehow connected to me or as comment about me that I have no place to stand in order to look at things objectively."

We apply brakes, therefore, by talking as if stressful situations were problems outside us to be solved. In large part they are. Losing a loved one is a very inward event. Our heart is touched. We do not solve this problem in the same way we might solve a problem with our car.

But there can and should be similarities. Someone's death is an event that happens around us, not just to us. While felt within, it is also an event outside us, one that needs to be experienced in part as an event in the world for which we must make arrangements and adjustments. Communicating objectively about our depressive situations moves us beyond feeling our pain to managing our problems.

Stop Holding On When You Need to Let Go

There are times in our struggle with depression when the wisest thing to do is to stop holding on and just let go. This may mean letting go of situations and giving them to parishioners. It may mean letting go and relying on an outside consultant.

More personally, it may mean letting go of our pastoral duties. Reverend Joberg, whom we also met in chapter 2, needed to do this. Suffering from disturbed self-identity, he was temporarily unfit to provide leadership. Refusing to let go of pastoral duties in this condition would likely have caused further distress for himself and others.

Even more critically, letting go may mean letting go of being the daily director of one's life. We may need to turn over to others decisions about our activities and care. This is not abdication. It is preservation of our embattled self.

Reverend Esling, unfortunately, was unable to do this. Rather than help himself by transferring responsibility for his care to family members and appropriate others, he left them compelled to enact this role. Reverend Esling missed an opportunity to share in his own recovery by letting others be in charge. He also missed an opportunity to reduce the guilt and consternation of his caretaking family. When over-whelmed, we can put brakes on depressive situations by letting go rather than holding on.

Finally, throughout the whole course of our depression, we assist ourselves by letting go to God. Situations are al-ways more bearable when we offer them up to our Creator. Even though we are clergy, this is often hard to do. One minister sounded a theme common to many of us, "I'd rather try to be in control than to trust." With that sentiment, we miss a spiritual opportunity to apply brakes to our depression. Indeed, with that sentiment we may have ushered in depression itself.

MEANINGS

Meanings are the lenses of life. Every situation is perceived through various lenses of meaning unique to each of us. Unfortunately, some of our lenses are distorted. Our meanings cause us to see ourselves and situations in depressing ways. A vicious circle ensues: distorted meanings induce depressive reactions, which reinforce distorted meanings, which amplify depressive reactions. Applying brakes on our unhealthy ways of giving meaning keeps depression from expanding. It is also a first step toward developing lenses that better honor life.

Stop Self-deprecations

1. Cease calling yourself names. No longer refer to yourself as "loser," "stupid," "weak," or "worthless." Bite your tongue.

2. Cease putting down your abilities, efforts, values, or faith. When depressed we are inclined to say, "I guess I wasn't cut out for ministry"; "My faith just wasn't strong enough"; or "There's probably something terribly sick at the core of my personality." Although truth may lurk in these statements, they are not introspections but indictments. These negative meanings distort rather than clarify.

3. Cease making disparaging comparisons with others. The key here is *disparaging*. Some comparisons challenge our depression. Seeing people worse off than we are can shock us back to reality. Observing how individuals cope with difficulties similar to our own can inspire us. But comparisons that deprecate are injurious. "I'm not as good as " or "I'm just as bad as" statements are meaning orientations that

erode the spirit. Although rationalized at times as ways of motivating ourselves, their net effect is to empower negative images and fuel depression's flame.

4. Cease excessive self-blame. Inappropriate guilt, unlike healthy guilt, does not seek repentance. It seeks punishment. It seeks castigation for one's shameful weakness. Such guilt pulls us down instead of building us up.

Be especially vigilant for self-blame that attributes *all* problems to one's self. "Everything I touch or try to do ends up wrong," said one depressed pastor. "It's me. I'm the problem. Everything boils down to being my fault." Research indicates that this tendency to find the meaning of all problems in one's self is a key ingredient for the onset of depression. At the stage of applying brakes, we cannot correct this type of thinking. We can, however, interrupt the articulation that gives false validation to this picture of our self.

Stop Distorting Your History

1. Abstain from misrepresenting the past. Quit being an unreliable narrator of yesterday. When depressed, we retroactively falsify. We look back on yesterdays and give them inappropriate meanings. On the one hand, we may see our past as more wonderful than it was, a golden age in comparison with our current state. On the other hand, we may see our past as worse than it was, nothing but an extension of our present misery. Neither does us service. Nostalgia over our golden age or rewriting our past with depressive ink adds burden to our melancholy.

2. Abstain from misrepresenting the present. Cease giving distorted meanings to the current story of your life. When depressed, we may "catastrophicize." We give crisis meanings to our present circumstances. Rather than declare that a certain situation is but a painful footnote in our present story, or at the most a painful paragraph, we claim that it is a painful

chapter in our life. Stressful episodes are responded to as critical trauma.

Furthermore, we may "globalize" this catastrophic event. We assert that *everything* in our present is affected by that trauma. Nothing remains untainted. As a result, the role and importance of other life events suffer. Present gloom artificially thickens.

These tendencies to catastrophicize and globalize have also been found to be key ingredients for the onset of depression. Applying brakes on these ways of giving meaning curbs our depression significantly.

3. Abstain from misrepresenting the future. Stop foreclosing your tomorrows. We may also "permanentize." "It will always be like this. For years to come, nothing will ever change I'm destined to suffer this way." We seal our future. Nothing new or healing is feasible because our misery is permanent.

This way of giving meaning also induces depression. Applying brakes on it keeps our depression in check while preserving our hope for new possibilities.

Stop Idolatry

1. Curtail overidealizing. Discontinue giving meanings that misplace ultimate power and hope. When we're depressed, we may turn people, things, or acts into idealized objects. We infuse them with special abilities and powers for the purpose of holding on to them for our own security. This is normal and helpful when kept within bounds.

But we tend to overidealize. We elevate people, things, and acts into the status of saving objects. Then we fantasize that they will rescue us from our helplessness if we follow their advice, possess them, or act like them. Depressed individuals often resort to adulation of charismatic figures and groups, about which we read so much.

We depressed pastors are no exception. We use a wealthy parishioner, a prized award, or a repeated ritual as an idealized object that we expect will infuse us with strength and deliver us from our despair. One minister became infatuated with a female parishioner whom he considered attractive and vivacious. In dangerously inappropriate ways he caressed that relationship, fantasizing that he could find in her a safe haven and the source of renewed vitality.

Such overidealizing leads to disillusionment. Our earthly saving objects always disappoint, leaving us even more depressed. We *do* need to find strong figures to lean on, but without transforming them into our saviors. We apply brakes to our depression by refusing to infuse objects with overidealized meaning.

2. Curtail excessive self-aggrandizement. Cease imposing inappropriate grandiose meanings on your own self.

Part of healthy self-esteem is deeming ourselves special and feeling entitled. But when depressed, we may over-aggrandize ourselves. We may expect others to consistently applaud us, follow our lead, or defer to us. One pastor demanded that everyone address him as "Reverend" because he had been uniquely called by God to be God's representative. Although his tone was confident, he, like many other narcissistic pastors, was attempting to ward off feelings of vulnerability by acting as if he were exceptional.

This form of idolatry seldom works. Grandiose efforts exhaust us. Inevitably we become disappointed in others. Our actions also push people away, leaving us even more isolated. Applying brakes on grandiose meanings protects our self-esteem and our supportive ties with significant individuals.

3. Curtail divesting God of power. Keep your religious head on straight. When depressed, we may become idolatrous by discrediting the meanings we have found in God. We may depreciate God's healing work. We may withdraw hope that comes from God. We may doubt God's reality.

Furthermore, we may give up on familiar religious practices, decrying them as no longer helpful. Here we regress to using religious practices only as functions that serve us, rather than embracing them as occasions to express the sacredness of our God-given life.

Divesting significance from God and our religious practices is risky business. Our religious meanings anchor our hope. They defend us against depression's sway.

We apply brakes by warding off such negative conclusions about God's presence and power. We apply brakes as well by refusing to alter the foundations of our faith and the meaningful ways of our worship. Keep acting the Christian's part, even if you don't feel like it. As Paul says, "hold fast to what is good" (1 Thessalonians 5:21).

BODY

Our depression is always embodied. The struggles of our soul incarnate themselves in our physical flesh. But our body instigates, not merely demonstrates. Our body can generate depression. Our body can amplify depression once it has started. It may do both. Not all of our depression is bodily induced, but there is no part of our depression that is not bodily involved. We participate in our recovery when we apply brakes to ways we handle our body.

Stop Immobility

Keep your body moving. Keep walking, bending, and stretching. Keep exercising. Maintain physical strength and stamina.

Depression retards our mobility. We want to lie still. We want to do little. If we do, we become physically weak. We tire easily. When that happens, depression grows. Tired bodies cannot deal with depressive situations. Tired bodies cannot think about distorted meanings.

Tired bodies also find it difficult to hope. Hope erodes when our body is exhausted. Hope is not just spiritually based, it is also physically based. It tends to dwindle in proportion to our waning physical strength.

Maintaining our energy level by staying mobile aids recovery. Keeping our muscles strong helps us keep our spirit strong.

Stop Physical Imbalances

Resist throwing your body off balance. Confront imbalances that already exist.

1. Eat right. Stick to balanced meals even though you don't feel like eating. Drink adequate fluids. Limit alcohol, strong coffee, and other substances that may put you on edge or cause you to feel down.

2. Rest. Your body battles not only normal exertions but also fatigue from your depression. Even if you can't sleep, go to bed rather than prowl the house. If you can't lie still, find a place where you can at least be physically quiet. Inhale deeply three times, and then hold your breath for as long as you can. This tends to make you yawn and aids relaxation. Use sleeping medication your doctor may prescribe. Consult a sleep specialist who can suggest alternative sleep rhythms and other sleep aids. In mild cases, all you may need to overcome your depression is adequate rest.

3. Get into the light. Your body needs brightness. Even if your gloom prefers the dark, walk in the daylight. Feel the sun. Increase the illumination in your workplace or home. Check with doctors about special lamps that can help with light-deprivation.

4. Take antidepressants if necessary. Adhere to medical advice about curtailing chemical imbalances in your body that spur your depression. Check your family history for depression and depression-causing illnesses. Work with medical specialists on ways to minimize conditions you may have inherited. Consider electroconvulsive therapy as a legitimate means for restoring balance in your whole system.

Stop Impulses

Curtail bodily impulses prompted by depression. Don't let your body dictate how much you eat, drink, or sleep, for example. Beware of sexual fantasies and desires that suddenly appear. Guard against the body's readiness to do anything to ward off feelings of deadness or tenseness.

Most important, control your body when suicidal impulses arise. At the stage of applying brakes, keeping your body from acting against you is more crucial than getting your thinking straight.

When necessary, treat you body as an object you must dominate. Don't feel embarrassed to say: "No, hands! You will *not* reach for those pills," or "No, feet! You will *not* walk to the garage." Don't hesitate to command: "Yes, fingers, you *will* dial for help," or "Yes, lips, you *will* share your temptation." Brake your body's impulse to harm you.

The renewal task of applying brakes is not gentle. I give pastors who come to me for therapy the same assertive suggestions you read in this chapter. I do so in order to convey just how crucial applying brakes is. I want to help pastors become tougher *with* themselves rather than harder *on* themselves. Depression can be like cancer. It can spread to new areas while feeding on itself. When this happens, we must be ruthless in confining it. Apply brakes.

Chapter Six

Holding Still

Dear God, put a patient spirit within us pastors. Help us learn to wait for strength before trying to run. Amen.

Convalesce. That's our second renewal task. Now that we have done the emergency work of braking our depression, we need a period of recuperation. We still hurt. We are still depressed. But now we try to maintain a state of equilibrium in situations, meanings, and body that will allow us to regain our strength.

The importance of this convalescing time has not been adequately recognized. In fact, getting depressed individuals back into the normal swing of things has been touted as the best medicine for their recovery. Such medicine does not always match an individual's need, however.

From my work with depressed pastors a recurring order emerges. They stop their downward slide but do not get back into the normal swing of things. They enter a holding pattern. They move neither forward nor backward. Their depression neither increases nor subsides.

Are these pastors stuck? Some may be. Most, however, appear to be at rest. This in-between period seems to be a natural phase in the healing process during which clergy are convalescing. While lamenting occasionally about not getting better, they actually begin to regain strength.

We depressed pastors can help ourselves by intentionally joining this phase of our recovery. Our renewal task can become that of *holding still*.

Holding still is not like going to bed. We do not convalesce by doing nothing. But we do become more thoughtful about our style and pace of life. Our dominant aim is to create around us and within us an environment conducive to recuperation so that emotional, physical, and spiritual energies can return.

Holding still is not easy to do. First, there is no public recognition of the need for holding still. Convalescing may seem indulgent. Second, we pastors feel obligated to carry out our duties fully. Others depend on us, emotionally and financially. Third, when we're depressed, we're inclined to flee to health. Anxious about not feeling normal, we push prematurely to resume our former activities.

Consequently we may commit the error of "too-soon-ness." We stop our therapeutic talks with others too soon. We stop taking our antidepressant medication too soon. We return to regular schedules too soon. We start making major decisions too soon. We may come out of the hospital too soon. We try to run as we once did before we are able. When these things happen, we frequently regress.

We need a period of convalescence to restore our resources. Holding still allows us to gather ourself together for the long walk home.

Guidelines for holding still:

1. Reevaluate the leading cause(s) of your depression. See if they have changed since applying brakes. Determine whether you need to hold still primarily with situations, meanings, or body processes.

2. Request assistance from those helping you. Explain to them about the process of holding still. Specify exactly what you will do to hold still and how they can support your efforts. Give them permission to call you to account when you exceed holding-still limits.

3. Stay wise when faced with people who react as if you're well. Seeing you mobile, people may expect you to be fully functional when in reality you are still among the walking wounded. You may be tempted to fulfill those expectations. Don't. Maintain the limits of your holding-still program.

4. Stay in a holding-still posture until you have your legs under you. There is no definite way to determine this. I myself have been guilty of nudging depressed pastors out of the holding-still stage before they were ready. Assess your progress carefully with those helping you.

5. Time, in any case, is not the gauge. Because some pastors are less depressed, they will move through this phase quickly. Others of us will require a longer time. Remember that you can always return to this task if you've moved forward, or if a helper has nudged you forward too soon.

6. Remind yourself that your holding still is an act of faith. In holding still we are actively waiting for the Lord. Like dry bones, we position ourselves for God's breath, waiting to be breathed into life again. Hope returns, however slowly, when we imagine ourselves faithfully joining God's healing plan.

SITUATIONS

Reverend Merrill had done well applying brakes to his depression. He had ceased keeping everything to himself. He had found safe company with whom he could express his feelings and evaluate his approaches. He was ready now for a period of recuperation.

His church, however, was not. The situation there deterio-rated. In addition to reduced attendance and giving, the congregation began to flounder in its meetings, neglect its building, and not pay its bills on time. Some committees even refused to meet in the church.

This raised serious questions for Reverend Merrill, as it would for any pastor. Is it possible to hold still in the midst of chaos? Can we convalesce while situations continue to be depressive? How can we deal with situations that both contribute to our depression and keep us from convalescing?

I urged Reverend Merrill to stay focused on his primary task. Working through his depression by joining the renewal process was his primary task. Overcoming his depression was not only personally important but also pragmatically indispensable. He could not be fully effective until he regained a sense of well-being. In short, he had to find ways to recoup while handling circumstances that were hard.

We worked out a strategy. First, we determined what actions he could take. We will discuss those in this section on situations. Second, we formulated what perspectives he could take. We will discuss those in our section on meanings. Finally, we devised what respites he could take. We will discuss those in our section on body. You my find these actions, perspectives, and respites useful in your own attempts to hold still. The aim, once again, is to establish an environment conducive to recuperation.

Practice Triage

Reverend Merrill's congregation was going through its own depression. Its lack of energy, dwindled motivation, inability to follow through, feelings of helplessness, and negative attitudes were all symptoms of depression. Even the church's lack of hunger for its customary meals together—an eating disturbance—signaled depression.

How could Reverend Merrill respond to the church's depression while being attentive to his own? How could he be effective and yet preserve time and energy for his own recuperation?

He could *practice triage*. Triage in medicine is the practice of sorting out and giving priority treatment to those who are most severely wounded. Reverend Merrill could do the same. To minimize the drain on his energy and time, Reverend Merrill needed to determine what issues were most important and what individuals were most injured.

That determination would take thought—and courage. Highlighted issues are not always the most serious. Loudest complainers are not always the most hurt. Pastors and I at this point pray our version of the serenity prayer, "God, grant us the wisdom to discern the more important from the less important and the courage to deal first with the former."

Once his priorities were determined, however, Reverend Merrill could direct his limited time and energy toward the most pressing wounds in his congregation. The tiring task of taking on the whole problem would thus be avoided.

To preserve himself further, Reverend Merrill could apply only lifesaving measures. The scope of his pastoral intervention would be limited. The most pressing issues and most injured individuals would receive emergency care. Exhaustive attempts to heal completely would thus be avoided.

Reverend Merrill's triage would regulate the extent of his involvement. It would allow him to be effective while still preserving room for his convalescence. As he eventually moved out of the holding-still phase, he could engage his congregation in more comprehensive ways. But at this stage getting fully into the normal swing of things would likely prove detrimental to him.

Set Boundaries

Triage limits the pastor's range of involvement in stressful situations. All too often, however, triage work becomes consuming. To avoid this, Reverend Merrill would also need to *set boundaries on his triage involvement.* For example, he could:

1. Block off specific hours to deal with issues and individuals rather than let them fill all his time.

2. Propose guidelines for how and when the congregation could formally address their problems.
3. Delegate tasks and share responsibilities with other church leaders.
4. Lean upon the guidance and management of outside consultants.

Reverend Merrill would also need to *set boundaries on his ruminations*. He might have successfully limited his action to triage. He might have successfully limited his involvement in the triage work itself. But he must also limit his ruminating about the church situation when not engaged in triage efforts.

When depressed, we pastors tend to lose control not only of our time but also of our thoughts. Concerns and worries fill our minds, expanding to every corner of our waking and sleeping. Our renewal task of holding still entails setting boundaries on our ruminations. For example, Reverend Merrill could do the following:

1. He could determine specific times outside triage work for unleashing his ruminations. Whenever unsolicited thoughts about the church arose, he could say to himself, "I'll not entertain those thoughts now. I'll do it between 4:00 P.M. and 5:00 P.M. on Tuesdays and Thursdays." Or, "I'll give in to my thoughts only when I meet with those I've chosen to help me through my depression."
2. He could imagine plucking unsolicited thoughts out of his head and placing them on a deserted island far away. "Stay there," he might say. "I'll come and visit you when I am ready." Most likely he would have to repeat this exercise until these thoughts found a confining place of residence.
3. He could play through unsolicited thoughts. When such thoughts persisted, he could laugh and say to them, "Well, here you are again. Even though you're

going to hang around and try to bug me, I'm going to attend to others things anyway."
4. He could use medication. If unsolicited thoughts became obsessive, Reverend Merrill could seek relief through antidepressants.

Learning to set boundaries is learning to be less situation-dependent. None of us can remain unaffected by turbulent situations in our life. But if our time, emotions, and thoughts are dictated primarily by our situations then we are too situation-dependent. Situations, rather than our own selves, determine what we do and what we feel. Setting boundaries is a step toward being responsive to situations rather than controlled by them.

Reverend Merrill's situation may not be our situation. But we can use the same actions to help ourselves hold still. Practicing triage and setting boundaries are basic ways to deal with depressive situations when we need to recuperate. They help create a contained environment wherein difficult situations can settle down and our disturbed self can regain strength.

MEANINGS

Lenses of life. That's what we've called the meanings we live by. Our restricted or distorted lenses affect what we pastors remember, how we do our work, and how we regulate our emotions. They cause or contribute to our depression. They also interfere with our task of holding still. Altering our meanings rather than our situations may be primary for our convalescence.

A stressful situation was the leading cause of Reverend Merrill's depression. A limited way of perceiving meaning was a contributing cause. To reinforce his holding-still task, we talked about healthy meaning perspectives he could adopt. Each meaning perspective aids recuperation.

Adopt a Macro-meaning Perspective

Reverend Merrill worked from a *micro*-meaning perspective. He focused more on parts than wholes. He thought short-term more than long-term. He dealt more with functions than with processes. He worked through individuals more than groups. He endeavored to fix more than to heal. Meanings emerged from the close-at-hand and focused on the here-and-now. Stated another way, Reverend Merrill was cognitively nearsighted.

This micro-meaning perspective served him adequately most of the time. Attention to details and concern about the present were fortes of his ministry. Concreteness and conscientiousness were hallmarks of his character.

But when difficulties arose, this meaning perspective alone was insufficient. On the one hand, it limited his understanding. For example, he interpreted his church's difficulties as reactions based on misconceptions. He reasoned that parishioners were upset with his policy changes because they did not fully comprehend why they were necessary and that working harder at communicating would solve the problem. Although partially accurate, he failed to perceive the larger meanings represented by his parishioners' discontent.

On the other hand, standing alone in his micro-meaning perspective limited his support. Managing particulars made his life feel secure. Running things well determined his self-esteem. Praise for his efforts was the nourishment he sought from others. When his micro world malfunctioned, he had little else to turn to for solace. In response, Reverend Merrill simply lowered his head and worked harder.

As he became more depressed, his meaning perspective constricted even further. He withdrew into himself, where meanings become more personalized. He focused increasingly on details, so that meanings rose and fell with the pulse of the moment.

How could Reverend Merrill help himself? By adopting a *macro*-meaning perspective. He needed to lift his head, look out, and behold a larger picture. Seeing his church as a whole self, for example, could help him understand the deeper pains the church was suffering. Seeing the church in historical perspective could inform him about its habitual ways of responding. Seeing the church as a system interacting with other systems could supply him with new meanings about community life.

Just as important, a macro-meaning perspective could bring reassurances. Not everything reflected on him. Not everything was controllable. He needed breathing space. He needed to push the world back a little and take refuge in seeing himself and his work in larger contexts of meaning.

For example, the ghosts of pastors past shape congregations—for good or ill. Church families transfer private struggles into parish life. Local economics and cultural attitudes create ecclesiastical vibrations. The state of the world—its political and environmental health—impacts upon the faith of congregations.

Reverend Merrill needed to place himself within this broader meaning perspective. Even to see himself and his congregation within the wide sweep of time and the vastness of space could bring sobering wisdom.

Holding still is aided by a macro-meaning perspective. Taking a larger view helps us become healthily detached. Our problems are pared down, or at least seen from a new perspective. Our efforts are altered, or at least our understanding is. Recovery from depression itself can then be seen as a long journey rather than a spontaneous remission.

Detachment does not mean inaction. Looking at the whole eventually allows us to deal better with the parts. Detachment is more a sage attitude born of seeing through the lens of larger meanings. We depressed pastors need this macro-meaning perspective for our task of holding still.

Adopt a Micro-meaning Perspective

Holding still is also difficult when one clings only to a *macro*-meaning perspective. For example, one denomina-tional leader thought more about ends than means. He re-flected more on historical time than personal time. He focused on *the laity* more than individual parishioners and on the universal church more than the local church. He spoke more of the *kingdom to come* than the *kingdom that is*. He observed more than participated.

When he became depressed, his macro world began to dissolve. Ideas seemed like abstractions. His visions seemed like fantasies. Future possibilities felt unreal and unattain-able. Desperately he tried to cast his net wider, to think and act even more expansively as a remedy for his malaise. It did not work.

What he needed was to be more grounded. He needed to adopt a *micro*-meaning perspective, through which he could find value and firmness in everyday earthiness, in what another pastor called "the thick soup of life." His convales-cence required looking for meaning in the preciousness of the moment, discovering it in each droplet of experience, and affirming it in the graciousness of simple acts.

Holding still is aided by a micro-meaning perspective. Focusing on particulars steadies us. Embracing the present centers us. Such grounding enables our convalescence.

Reverend Merrill and the denominational pastor repre-sent extremes of the micro- and macro-meaning perspec-tives. A wide range exists between these two. The renewal task of holding still requires us clergy to establish a balance between these perspectives so that each sustains, and re-strains, the other.

Adopt a Theo-meaning Perspective

Augustine exposes our need, "Our hearts are restless until they find their rest in thee." Our rest at the holding-still phase also requires a theo-meaning perspective. We must strive to see life in the light of God. We must strive to maintain a spiritual meaning perspective through which, with reverent imagination, we sense God's presence and affirm God's work.

A theo-meaning perspective instills hope. We discover more than we found in our micro and macro worlds. God is *in* them. God is *over* them. Reverend Merrill's church is God's church, just as his daily life is in God's hands. The denominational leader's visions are under God's purview, just as the whole sweep of history is under God's domain. Even through our depression God is working out God's purposes. Each experience has a halo of meaning when perceived through a divine lens.

We can hold still more assuredly if we attune our hearts to God. We can hold still more calmly if we perceive ourselves to be held by God. Our state of rest can become an act of faith when we perceive through a theo-meaning perspective.

BODY

In general, depressed pastors adequately maintain their bodies. Although melancholy, they know that the body is like a dog. If you mistreat it, it snarls. Reverend Merrill, for example, tried to eat properly, even though his appetite had dwindled. He sought rest although restless. He endeavored to exercise although lacking motivation. Only with severely depressed clergy have I needed to help them apply brakes to their neglect of body needs.

Depressed pastors do less well repairing their bodies. They tend to ignore signs of physically related problems. They are reluctant to go for medical tests. They do not consistently follow medical advice. Throughout these chapters, we have highlighted the need for proper medical attention for physical problems that may be causes or consequences of depression.

Depressed pastors also do less well convalescing through their bodies. Creating a state of equilibrium in the body that allows for recuperation of energies is somewhat unusual for them. Beyond knowing the need for time to unwind, they have limited experience holding still through their body.

Convalescing calls for *respites*. Pastors need to find ways to hold still bodily. Jesus gives guidance for doing this.

Jesus was remarkably body-conscious. He lived through the fullness of his body. He responded to each person as a body-self and healed each person as a body-self. He embraced the body as intrinsic to spiritual life and emotional solace. Two examples from Jesus suggest ways to respite through our body.

Relocate Your Body

The apostles gathered around Jesus, and told him all that they had done and taught. He said to them, "Come away to a deserted place all by yourselves and rest for a while." For many were coming and going, and they had no leisure even to eat.

(*Mark 6:30-32*)

These words were a directive for the beleaguered disciples. They are also words for us when we are overwhelmed. Jesus knew the need for solitude, a time away from the push of the milling crowd so that one's body-self can be renewed. Breathless life needs breathing spaces. Relocating our body away from hectic environs allows physical and spiritual convalescence.

Jesus followed his own advice. The morning after a frantic day of healing the sick, Jesus got up "while it was still very dark . . . and went out to a deserted place, and there he prayed" (Mark 1:35). When grieved over the death of John the Baptist, "he withdrew from there in a boat to a deserted place by himself" (Matthew 14:13). This habit of relocating his body-self to a deserted place was a convalescing act of Jesus. He knew the need for solitude, especially when his spirit was troubled.

Each occasion of solitude brought more than solace to Jesus. It brought strength. Deserted-place experiences were followed by new waves of compassion for the people seeking him. Relocating our body to deserted places allows us eventually to be more involved. Solitude fosters restored empathy as we convalesce from our depression.

If I could direct the lives of depressed pastors for three days, I'd have them go to a deserted place where they could do nothing but eat and sleep. I suspect that many depressive tensions would be eased by three days of peaceful rest and good nutrition.

How could Reverend Merrill find respite through relocation? We talked about this. He began by saying he felt selfish looking for times of solitude. He also felt strange. And yet deep down he yearned for solitude. It called to him.

He knew that finding solitude in his office was an unlikely prospect. Work would distract him. He came up with the idea of driving out to the countryside regularly to walk in the woods. He also contemplated spending time at a nearby monastery in semi-seclusion. Although he had to arrange for them, he began to look forward to his own occasions of solitude.

Each of us can devise our own respite of relocation. The key is distancing ourselves physically from our present environment. This act of holding still is not a mental act, a retreat into our own thoughts. It is a body act in which you go away to a deserted place all by yourself and rest for a while.

Vent Your Body

Jesus vented. He released the emotions and tensions that built up within his body. He wept. He acted out his love. He showed his temper. He displayed his fright.

Jesus demonstrated healthy catharsis. Although he vented his feelings to serve other purposes, he modeled how expressing our feelings keeps our body-self vibrant. He never assumed that God would have us be placid servants who never give expression to all the surging passions and feelings welling up within us.

As we have seen, Reverend Merrill bottled up tensions and emotions. This was a contributing cause of his depression. To help his convalescence, we explored ways to vent his body besides talking to safe company. We especially focused on venting the negative body tensions that kept him agitated. Since he was not comfortable with a respite approach, we thought first of gentle ventings.

One possibility was imaging. "Imagine that the heaviness of your depression has turned to liquid and is pouring out your fingers. You can feel it, pouring, gushing out your fingers, flowing all over on the floor and immediately evaporating, leaving you feeling more lighthearted than you've been in a long time." Relaxation exercises of this nature can help depressed clergy hold still through their body.

Another possibility was being touched. Hugging purges us of toxic poisons. Sexual intimacy drains stress. A professional massage can ease anxieties. Also, the touch of warm whirlpool water and hot sauna steam can melt the sludge around our hearts.

Still another possibility was action. Therapeutic techniques, like pounding a pillow or yelling at an empty chair (where the object of our agitation symbolically sits), release tensions. Moderate to strenuous exercise works out body stress. Expressing righteous indignation by taking a stand not only gets things off our chests but actually fortifies our wills.

Our culture provides many methods for body-self cathar-sis. Depressed pastors should choose those suited to their individual personalities. They should also select methods that maintain their integrity. Not all ways of venting emulate Jesus.

While Reverend Merrill and I were talking about holding still through the body, he remembered how a parishioner had ministered to him through her own approach to her body. She had said to him, "I have cancer, but I chose not to see myself as struggling with cancer. I chose to see this as a journey into a new phase of my life." God provides many opportunities for learning body peace.

CHAPTER SEVEN
Returning Home

Dear God, thanks to you we're beginning to feel normal again. Help us act in ways that will further restore our former sense of self. Amen.

We're coming out of the valley. Applying brakes has halted our slide down rocky slopes. Holding still has allowed us to nurse our wounds and garner strength. Now we find ourselves moving decidedly upward. The grass seems greener, the air cleaner. There's a sun in our emotional sky, working its way through our clouds. Over the ridge we see again the church's spire, and like European travelers of generations past, we turn toward it for guidance.

Our old self is returning. We are beginning to feel normal, a state once so familiar to us that we took it for granted. Now we count it a blessing. We never knew what we had until we lost it.

If asked to describe what we've lost, we would probably say something like, "I haven't felt like my self. I've lost part of me." In chapter 2 we called this loss of our normal sense of self *the loss of self-cohesion.* Our self has fallen apart to some degree. It has fragmented. Our symptoms of depression are signs that our self's firmness, its cohesion, has deteriorated. The *levels of self-disturbance* identified in chapter 2 indicate the extent to which we can lose our hold on our self.

As we heal, the signs of depression begin to lift, which means we are regaining our self-cohesion. Our predepression self is being restored. Self-righting mechanisms within us cycle us home. We notice this when we're in a decent mood again, when our self-confidence returns, or when our convictions seem vital once more. We notice this when we begin to function better again, to regain our identity, or to reassume adequate control of our personal lives. The return of our old self signals the restoration of our self-cohesion.

This description sounds impersonal. But when you feel it in your body—when you feel what it's like to lose hold of your self through depression and how wonderful it is to regain that sense of self—then you know personally the reality of lost and restored self-cohesion.

Restore self-cohesion. This is our third renewal task. We join the movement toward our normal self by *returning home*, by trying to recover our lost self-cohesion. More specifically, we attempt to deal with stressful situations, meanings, and body processes in ways that reestablish our sense of self.

Ironically, those of us in the helping professions tend to minimize this return home. Why? Because we tend to *look beyond* returning home. We strive to help depressed individuals *become better* than they were rather than *recover* their former sense of self.

For example, when Reverend Merrill first came to see me he said, "I feel as if I'm coming unglued. Nothing seems right anymore." This was his personal way of expressing the loss of his self-cohesion, the loss of his habitual way of feeling inside. What he yearned for was some way to feel better. Feeling better meant to feel like his old self again. It did not mean becoming a better self.

Although I knew that, I still kept *thinking change.* I looked for areas in which he needed to develop more adequate self-cohesion. I looked for what he could and should become.

All of us need to improve. But that was not Reverend Merrill's desire, nor what he needed. He was yearning to be himself again, and rightly so. Work on self-recovery is as vital as work on self-improvement.

In fact, our daily effort to retain our habitual level of self-cohesion is the more common dynamic in our life. We constantly strive to *feel normal* inside, to *feel like ourselves*— whatever the nature of that self-cohesion might be. These efforts to preserve ourselves are more ordinary than efforts to change ourselves.

We pastors now have the capacity to work on this renewal task. No longer needing simply to protect ourselves (apply-ing brakes) or convalesce (holding still), we are able to em-bark on the journey to restore ourselves (returning home). We still feel vulnerable. We know the path stretches far ahead. But moments of normality reassure us. Relief from constant stress uplifts us. Anticipation of victory fires our spirit.

Guidelines for returning home:
1. Reassess the causes of your depression. At this stage of recovery, attention should focus on contributing causes as well as leading causes.
2. While taking on normal activities aids recovery of nor-mal feelings, you will want to experiment with various ways to regain your self-cohesion. Do not base your return home simply on getting back into the swing of things.
3. Remember to focus primarily on restoring your *old self* before striving to become a *new self.* At this stage we are not looking down the road of life asking ourselves where we want to be when we come to the end of our journey. We are looking down the road to find that familiar place we experienced before depression took us into a strange land. In short, honor the healing process.
4. Stay connected with those who support you and hold you accountable. This is no time for a solo journey.

Being surrounded by empathic others is essential for firm self-cohesion throughout life. Those relationships are especially important when our cohesion needs mending.

5. Finally, remember the spiritually obvious: It is in loving and serving God that we find our true cohesion. Returning home comes ultimately through having a heart for God, walking daily with Jesus, and responding sensitively to the needs of others.

SITUATIONS

Depressive situations tend to make us feel helpless. We become overwhelmed to some degree by events that seem beyond our control. Confidence to handle situations dwindles. Physical and spiritual muscles weaken.

To regain our self-cohesion *experienced as feeling empowered*, we must counteract this mood of helplessness. Over the years I have suggested various approaches to stressful situations that can help pastors feel empowered. These are not specifically religious acts. They are in the mode of what we might call *practical spirituality*, practical efforts to preserve God's central gift to us—our self.

Aggress Plans

Self-cohesion returns when we devise a fitting plan of action and carry it out aggressively. This is more than the applying brakes act of *not turning away* and the holding still act of *triage*. This is an all-out, *taking-it-on* approach through which, with a forceful spirit, we put into operation an appropriate strategy.

I say to pastors working on their returning-home task: "What can you do to resolve your depressive situation? Confront it. Make a plan. Helplessness feeds on indecisiveness. But yours can't be just any plan. It has to fit. That means it must be realistic; it must honor the situation; and it must demonstrate your integrity." Devising skillful plans instills confidence. Acting with character instills morale.

I also urge pastors to arouse *the sleeping giant.* I say to them: "In spite of how helpless you might feel, there is a giant in you. You are bigger, stronger, and braver than you think. Find that giant. Wake it up. Let it stand up tall. Let it flex its muscles and even be ferocious at times if it needs to be. Be that giant as you carry out your plan." Helplessness fades when we stand hands-on-hips, glaring at our situation with shrewd designs in mind.

This is not a metaphor for males only. Female clergy, too, need to see themselves fighting the good fight with brawn and brains. Indeed, denying female clergy these empower-ing self-images may leave them vulnerable to depression.

Evoke Feelings

Self-cohesion returns when we embrace our emotions and the emotions of others. Conversely, withdrawing from our feelings expands our sense of helplessness.

One pastor found herself "absolutely without any pri-mary relationships in my life. My only connection with other people is when I'm serving them. But there's nobody for me to turn to, nobody who can hold me or make love to me."

In an effort to protect herself, she blunted her feelings. "It's too painful to feel my own loneliness. And it's too over-whelming to feel what other people are going through, whether good or bad."

After a period of applying brakes and holding still, we sought to restore her self-cohesion by having her fully evoke her feelings. Rather than being a passive recipient, she delib-erately granted a place to her feelings. She called them to her to acknowledge them, name them, own them, and learn from them.

104

It was not easy. But being in touch with her own emotional core gradually revitalized her. She felt whole again. She felt courageous. She felt a deeper empathy for her self and her situation. Resonating with the emotions of others also revitalized her. She regained close ties. Her empathy for others expanded, and she moved from mere serving to genuine caring.

Bringing our feelings close to our heart fortifies our sense of self. This is not a prescription for females only. Male clergy also need to reconnect to feelings as the basis for well-being. Denial of this need has ushered many male pastors to the brink of depression—and often cast them in.

Impose Interpretations

Self-cohesion returns when we assign situations a meaning and place within our mental, emotional, and spiritual world. Imposing interpretations constrains the devastating impact of situations that render us weak.

For example, pastors often feel reassured at the onset of counseling by my interpretations about causes of depression and the nature of renewal tasks. They experience their own empowerment when constructing their own interpretations along the way. Describing, defining, and mentally positioning stressful situations aid cohesion.

One pastor shared with other clergy his panic at having to deal with his church's reactions to the sexual misconduct of his predecessor. The group empathized with his difficulty but urged him to *make sense* of this situation in ways that could strengthen him. With their help he began to formulate theological and psychological interpretations about his pastoral circumstance and the impact on his own sexuality. In so doing, the overwhelming nature of the whole mess began to dissipate. The situation gradually took on structure as he became fortified with interpretative meanings. As a result, his sense of helplessness shrank and his sense of cohesion grew.

Imposing interpretations is one of the most formidable powers God gives us. With it we can order, unify, transform, and redeem. With it we can distort and spiritually kill. Use this power with caution, but use it.

Pronounce Evaluations

Self-cohesion returns when we confirm or deny the cir- cumstances of our situation. In this approach we counter helplessness with an evaluative stance.

In the very best sense of the phrase we *get on our high horse.* This does not mean to speak with condescension. It means to speak with a voice that says "yea" or "nay," that gives a strong stamp of approval or a judgmental word of criticism. It is a stance that boldly points a finger and either calls attention to a person deserving public acclaim or calls to account behavior that needs correction if not censure.

Taking a moral stance is not only a consequence of strength; it is a source of strength. Righteous indignation fires our soul. Righteous praise sparks our spirit. Our weakened selves regain cohesion when we pronounce evaluations.

You may already practice one of these four approaches. Use it again, but also expand your repertoire. Experiment with other approaches. Integrate them with your habitual mode of reestablishing self-cohesion.

Meanings

While depressive meanings can also produce helpless- ness, they primarily create feelings of worthlessness. For example, deeming ourselves weak because we are unable to push away dark moods pulls down our self-respect. Imagin- ing that we are victims of melancholy, or that others see our depression as deserved, wears away our self-regard.

To regain our self-cohesion *experienced as positive self-esteem*, we must counteract this mood of worthlessness. One approach for promoting healthy self-feelings is to continue to confront depressive meanings. Another approach is to engage fully in the process of finding and giving meaning. In this chapter we consider the latter.

Learn

"I want a PhD in *me*," one pastor announced as his goal for counseling. As we laughed about and then explored this, it became clear that his desire to learn served the purpose of shoring up his self-esteem. "When I understand something I feel more competent, and when I feel more competent I feel better about myself."

Research suggests that our self-esteem is based on our sense of being competent, and learning is a primary way we come to feel more competent. That learning may come through instruction, observation, intuition, critical reflection, or imagination. Whatever the mode, learning makes not only a path for us to walk on, it also makes us self-confident walkers. Gaining understanding can verify our ability to perceive and reason wisely. It can enhance our capacity to manage our self and our situations.

Learning builds self-esteem. This was true when we glowed with pride because we learned our ABCs or mastered how to find our way around the block. It remains true in our adulthood when we feel silently proud because we learn medical terms or master our way through life's maze of responsibilities. To possess knowledge and understanding is to feel good about our self. This is not necessarily egotism, although it can be. It is a natural way God provides for self-affirmation.

I urge pastors to intentionally learn as a means for restoring their self-cohesion experienced as positive self-esteem. Counseling itself can serve as a learning lab. Studying familiar scripture in light of our present condition can reveal undiscovered insights. Attending classes can equip us with additional skills. And understanding others can be one of the most caring yet self-benefiting acts of learning imaginable. We return home on a road paved with self-satisfied moments of having acquired understanding.

Teach

Self-cohesion experienced as positive self-esteem is also restored when we assist others in their search for meaning. Teaching, in whatever form it may take, blesses us as well as those we aid. For example, I'm able to work through my own depressive moods primarily by cultivating reflections in pastors. I feel useful, if not occasionally wise, when I'm able to offer a word that brings a joyful look of understanding or keeps flagging hope alive. On days when my self-cohesion is shaky, an hour of soul-searching therapy with a distressed pastor restores my equilibrium. Likewise, teaching a seminar on recovery from depression eases my own depressive tensions.

I encourage pastors to intentionally teach in order to return home. Sermons can become vital occasions for life instruction. Special seminars can offer useful information. Pastoral calls can illuminate faith. Pastoral counseling can clarify a person's life story, or prompt necessary revisions. We recovering pastors now have capacities to teach energetically rather than talk dejectedly. In so doing, we satisfy the hunger of parishioners for understanding and our own hunger for feeling worthwhile.

Always, of course, we must remain mindful of our limitations as assistants to understanding. A silent prayer weaves through my work to keep me rightly oriented:

> If their guide I'm called to be,
> Let these pastors clearly see.
> The counselor leaning hard on Thee.

Our personal pride in teaching, however, is part of God's reward for work faithfully done. Let us not minimize this gift. It keeps us whole and protects us from the weariness of well-doing.

Seek to Be Understood

"I need to be understood. When I feel understood—when someone is tuned-in to what I'm doing and going through—then I feel that I'm a person who's taken seriously and even respected. I like praise, but what really makes me feel valued is someone caring enough to really know me."

Strikes a chord, doesn't it? We, too, yearn to be understood in ways that convey we are cared for if not cherished. To feel understood is to feel valued. To feel misunderstood or ignored is to feel invisible, of little significance, or downright unlikable.

Furthermore, being applauded without being understood is empty praise. Such applause seems superficial to us, or of only momentary delight. But when we feel deeply understood, we are filled with the conviction that the world around us is sending reassuring signals that our continued existence is meaningful and valued. Such acts of understanding sustain our worth and our will to carry on.

When depressed, we may seek to be understood in all the wrong places. Just ask a spouse injured by a depressed pastor's infidelity, for example. But our seeking to be understood is never wrong. In fact, it's a sign that we still have remnant strength to pursue what our fragmented self needs, namely the understanding of others that affirms our significance.

Is feeling understood only meaningful if it comes unsolicited from others? Not at all. If that were the case, then no person who enters counseling could ever be uplifted by the understanding of the counselor. Let's not be ashamed to ask for understanding from appropriate others. That's not begging. It's wisely seeking the responses we need. Furthermore, let us express ourselves openly so that others can empathize with what we are experiencing. Let us also help others adjust their understanding until they more adequately resonate with who we are. Finally, let us feel valued by the effort of others to understand us *even though they miss the mark.* Perceiving the desire of others to understand can be as gratifying to us as the accuracy of their understanding.

BODY

Body conditions that lead or contribute to depression may also instill helplessness ("I'm too weak to do anything"), or worthlessness ("I'm too weak to be of any good"). Such conditions, however, often instill hopelessness.

While hope is spiritual, its roots lie in the flesh. Our sense of life's reliability, predictability, and well-being is closely connected to the intactness of our body. When our body falters, so does our hope to some degree. Our future darkens. Optimism wanes. Promises lose credibility. There may seem less to rely on, less to trust. Even if we are healthy, all we have to do is step inside a nursing home to experience a blast to our implicit hopes for lifelong vigor and self-control.

If we are not depressed, a body shock to our innate hopefulness may provoke depression. "I've always kind of liked my body and trusted it," said one distressed pastor. "But since I found lumps in my breast and other strange things, I've changed. I battle my body now. It's the enemy. I don't trust it anymore. I don't know what's going on with me or what's going to happen next. Nothing feels secure."

If we are already depressed, we become even more susceptible to the impact of our body upon our hopefulness. "I'm really upset about this chemical imbalance" confided one pastor. "I'm glad there's something we can do for my depression, but I feel even more abnormal now. It's not just my emotions that aren't right. My *body's* not right. It's a shock to me. My whole world feels upside down."

To regain our self-cohesion *experienced as hopefulness,* we must counter this mood of hopelessness. One place where we can, even must, do this is through our relationship with our body. Peace of mind cannot be obtained by separating from our physical being. Returning home to a state of hope-fulness requires attentiveness to the very body that may induce our depression.

Work with Your Body

Hopefulness returns when we engage our bodies in the healing process. "I'm much calmer now," reported the pastor who battled her body. "Rather than fight my body I've started to collect data about it. I literally chart its various changes on a graph. I talk to my doctors about them and then we determine the best response. So I'm trying to work with my body and what it's going through rather than struggle against it. I feel a lot better doing that."

Working with her body restored her hopefulness as she anticipated being healed or at least stabilized. Working with her body rather than battling it also revitalized hope by reestablishing body-self unity. She was no longer at war with herself. In addition, hopefulness returned as she assumed a working role. She was not just doing something to help herself; she was *doing something.* Taking a step, sometimes any step, quickens a hopeless spirit.

Trust Your Body

Hopefulness also returns when we trust our body. On the one hand, we can trust that our body's symptoms are mes-sages to us requesting change. Our body alerts us to altera-tions we must make for our total well-being. If we are wise, we will heed them.

On the other hand, we can trust our body's own wisdom. Our body is drawn toward health. It corrects itself. It seeks livable compromises. It fights the good fight. Rather than ask, "Can the mind heal the body?" we can ask, "How can I let my body do what it does naturally without my mind getting in the way?" Hope returns when we place confidence in the self-righting mechanisms of our God-created body.

Live Your Body

Finally, our self-cohesion experienced as hopefulness returns when we live our bodies fully. When we're depressed, we amputate our bodies. We devalue them, treat them as objects, distance ourselves from body feelings, or actually try to escape from our bodies. This attempted alienation from the thickness of bodily life contributes to our sense of hopelessness. We are cut off from the ground of our existence and from all the security and vitality it affords us.

Returning home to hopefulness requires living our body fully. That means letting our bodily feelings come strong and forceful: letting our nerve endings tingle when listening to inspiring music; letting our hearts ache for those who suffer; or letting our whole body absorb the pleasure of a hug or the delight of sexual intimacy. It means running our fingers through the soil and knowing we are part of it. It means breathing in deeply the winds of the seasons and swaying in rhythm with the ebb and flow of life.

Living our body fully means using our body to know how others are experiencing life and how it feels to walk in their body-self with its dimensions, skills, limitations, and looks. It means bodily sensing what is right and wrong before our head comes to know and relying upon body reactions to what people say and do.

Living our body fully toward hopefulness means savoring the vigor as well as the decline that comes with aging. It means embracing the pains of our body that signal brokenness or rebirth of health. It means sensing our own deaths and greeting them from afar. It means honoring our body as an instrument of the Spirit through which God assures us we will never be alone.

This is not romanticizing the body. It's being responsive to the incarnation of our hope. Our body may not be cured but our self can be healed as we live our body fully.

We're coming out of the valley. Like the psalmist of old who made it up and over, we gaze back and see God's unfailing presence with us along the way. We're coming home, home to our normal self. Let us rejoice and give thanks!

CHAPTER EIGHT
Stepping Beyond

Dear God, help us wrestle a blessing from our depression. Since it has pulled us apart, may we use it to put our self together again better than ever. Amen.

What will you do when your depression lifts? Most pastors are like the one healed leper who returned with thanks. We're inclined to express gratitude to God and others for seeing us through the valley.

But then what? Is that all? Do we merely resume life again, mopping up the splatter of problems left by depression's wake? Let's hope not. Let's hope we will be determined to wrestle a blessing from our depression.

When depressed, we are distorted into shapes we lament. Using our depression, we should strive to be transformed into shapes we desire: more peaceful selves, more coura geous selves, and more understanding selves.

The end of recovery from depression terminates not with returning home but with *stepping beyond*. This is our fourth renewal task. Stepping beyond does not mean trying to put depression farther behind us. It means, instead, embracing our depression while memories are still fresh so we can step beyond into more of life. *What we become through depression, not how we defeat it, is of ultimate importance.*

Although depression can be a school for change, it is no teacher. Depression itself teaches us nothing. Depression has no inherent meaning. It does not, as some claim, generate its own style of awareness or brand of insight.

Instead, depression sets the stage for new life by fracturing our habituality. Depression violently works the soil of our heads and hearts. It breaks the ground of our customary thoughts and attitudes. The resulting fragmentation of our self creates new spaces in which new awareness can arise. It becomes possible to see shadows never clearly noticed and lights previously blocked from sight.

One particular way pastors and I attempt to step beyond is *by deepening our sense of the sacred.* We use our experiences of depression to enhance our spiritual awareness. More specifically, we attempt to discern the sacred in and through depression's effects on our situations, meanings, and body. Developing our sensitivity to the sacred was part of our work on other renewal tasks. Now it becomes our main quest.

Does one have to go through depression before one can expand one's sense of the sacred? Not at all. But distressing episodes are fertile opportunities for spiritual growth—if we don't weaken too much. Our good sense should not allow depression to yank us through hell without any attempt to convert it into a means of grace.

Two approaches are necessary for deepening our sense of the sacred. These are especially important when using our depression to step beyond.

First, we must search for the sacred. There are times when holy moments leap out unexpectedly. We are suddenly filled with awe. Searching for the sacred is less familiar. In searching, we actively make ourselves available for sacred encounters and even seek to induce them.

Second, we must use reverent imagination. This means a shift from perceiving things in mundane ways to perceiving things in spiritual ways. Reverently we imagine that the familiar may be more than what it looks like, and that the

115

sacred may be the familiar's hidden reality. Such reverent imagination produces more a sense we can feel than a content we can define, understanding more than truth.

How we derive a blessing from depression will be particular to each of us. How we might sense the sacred more deeply will also be particular to each of us. The following are experiences of pastors who found dwellings of the sacred in depression's altered landscape.

SACRED SITUATIONS

"It's amazing how depression shrinks life," said a postdepression pastor. "I spent a lot of downtime just drinking tea and staring at the leaves in the bottom of my cup."

Other ministers convey similar experiences: "I'd sit for long periods just looking at my hands or following every movement my wife made around the kitchen."

"The walls caved in until small things were my whole world. Every situation posed a threat or injured me. On the other hand, I clung to every situation to make me feel better or save me."

"It got so bad that about all I could do was say *yes* or *no*."

Depression reduces life to particulars. That's disturbing. A melancholy micro-world constricts our spirits. Although adopting a macro meaning perspective can be an antidote, as we discussed in our last chapter, this reduction to particulars itself can yield a blessing.

Some of us would probably admit that we are so busy with the details of daily ministry that we don't think about ultimates very much. But upon reflection, we would probably admit that we don't think about details very much either. We take the ordinary as ordinary. We look but don't pay close attention. We sleepwalk through life, much like the people Emily Gibbs cries out to in Thornton Wilder's play *Our Town*.

Dead from giving birth to her second child, Emily Gibbs comes down from her grave on the hillside above Grover's Corners to live once again her twelfth birthday. She enters the kitchen where her mother is fixing breakfast:

> Oh, Mama, just look at me one minute as though you really saw me. Mama, fourteen years have gone by. I'm dead . . . But, just for a moment now we're all together . . . *Let's look at one another.*[1]

But it doesn't happen. No one hears. No one really looks or sees. Life's moments continue to be passed over rather than embraced as precious. Finally Emily can bear it no longer. She breaks down in sobs:

> I didn't realize. So all that was going on and we never noticed. Take me back—up the hill—to my grave. But first: Wait! One more look.
>
> Good-by, Good-by, world. Good-by, Grover's Corners . . . Mama and Papa. Good-by to clocks ticking . . . and Mama's sunflowers. And food and coffee. And new-ironed dresses and hot baths . . . and sleeping and waking up. Oh, earth, you're too wonderful for anybody to realize you. Do any human beings ever realize life while they live it?—every, every minute?[2]

Through our depression we, too, can understand like Emily Gibbs. Depression is a form of death that opens us to new life. As our world shrinks and our customary mode of moving through it passes away, we are forced nose-to-nose with life's particulars. Depression rivets our eyes to the mundane. It holds our head so that we cannot turn away. The habituality of our perception is fractured. By shrinking our vision, depression exposes us to a world of detail.

And then, standing on our own hillside, looking down at the valley we've just left, we, too, may come alive to the new creation around us. In a spirit of wonder, we gaze afresh at life's particulars and cannot escape their singularity, their complexity, their mystery. Like Emily Gibbs, we discover the sacred in life's everydayness. We are awed by the beauty in nature's simplest form. We are stirred by the passion of life played out in the most mundane event. We are entranced by the magic of daily rituals, those ways of doing things that seem given, orderly, and secure. We are touched by the smallest act of kindness.

Once we waited for the sacred to invade our lives, but now with soul-filled Emily Dickinson we're inclined to claim the opposite: "Life is a spell so exquisite that everything conspires to break it."

When one is immersed in this reverent spirit, drinking tea is no longer just drinking tea. A spouse's movement is no longer just a spouse's movement. Saying *yes* or *no* is no longer just saying yes or no. Seeing everything from a new perspective, we come alive as Emily Gibbs yearns for us to do, and we begin to recognize the sacredness of life while we live it—every, every minute.

When that happens, we become better at being fully present in each situation. We are more inclined to embrace situations in an affirming, hopeful, trusting way. We feel inspired to reveal the sacred in each circumstance for the benefit of all.

Our spiritual life is not primarily about transcendence but about concrete immersions in the particulars of existence. With this new sense of the sacred, we see the boundary between us and the sacred become but a threshold. Sometimes the sacred leaps out at us surprisingly. Sometimes we step across expectantly. In any case, we are less inclined to skate across situations or sink in their morass, for we embrace our situations as tabernacles of the sacred.

"I've come to see how significant my tea drinking was," continued the pastor. "It not only grounded me, it opened me to the uncommon commonness of everyday objects and acts. It helped me realize how full of life mundane events can be. I fondly refer to this as 'having found the sacred in the teapot.'

"I look at things differently now A wave from someone passing by, the growth of my trees, even emptying waste-baskets at church are holy moments when I look at them with reverent understanding. And when I get anxious about a particular situation, I just respond as if it contains something of the sacred. Then I'm able to move on more confidently and peacefully."

Our soul is never far away from particulars. And God, indeed, is in those details.

SACRED MEANINGS

The late John Chancellor once said, "If you want to make God laugh, tell him your plans." Perhaps no other aspect of our life is more disrupted by depression than the world of meanings we live by and build from.

"It's hard to believe what I believed when I was de-pressed," reminisced one minister with a far-off look. "Those meanings that had always strengthened me seemed empty, even false. But you know, it wasn't just that the bottom fell out of my world. It was that I also began to concoct a world. I began to believe that I was worthless, and always had been, and that other people really didn't care for me but were just using me. Bizarre thoughts, fantasies, and premonitions filled my mind."

Not only do our debilitating thoughts generate depres-sion, our depression also generates debilitating thoughts. A malignant spiral often ensues. Negative thoughts lead to depressive thinking that reinforces negative thoughts. Our giving of meaning can become lethal, physically as well as spiritually. But even from this degeneration a blessing might

119

be won. Deep reflection in a spirit of reverent imagination can lead us to new understandings.

"I've always known intellectually that each of us sees the world from our own viewpoint," continued the pastor. "But for the first time I got in touch with something deeper. What struck me was that just as I concocted a distorted world of meanings when I was depressed, so, too, have I constructed an orderly world of meanings when I'm not depressed. I *create* a world around me. It's not just that I put my personal twist on reality. I *create* my reality. I project around me a complete scenario about what the world is, who I am, and what life is like.

"That's scary to realize. I've wanted to believe that the meanings I live by are simply out there to be grasped or that I just interpret the experiences that come to me. But I'm not sure anymore. After my bout with depression, I can't escape the thought that each of us *makes* our own lived world—for better or worse."

Depression can fracture the habituality of our thinking. The question of meaning-giving, which depression forces on us, erodes the facades of our reality. Struck by how we generated a fictive world when depressed, we begin to see that from the first day of our life to the last we create a meaning-world around us. We begin to realize that our meanings are not given to our minds by a concrete world, but are the products of our minds, which constantly construct worlds. "Where you are, there arises a place," observes the poet Rainer Maria Rilke. Human consciousness in all its contingency gives rise to the order and structure it claims merely to find.

From our depression we also realize how our meaning-world vacillates. Changes in our environment, mental status, and body's condition lead us to construct new realities, new worlds of meaning—for better or worse.

This fracturing of our habitual thinking can be upsetting. It can also open us to dwelling places of the sacred. Just as we were led to acknowledge the sacredness of life's particulars, so can we come to recognize the sacredness of our world-making.

"Even though it was dangerous, there was something sacred in that ominous power to create a distorted world when I was depressed," continued the pastor. "I fear my creativity, for it can go astray, but I also embrace its twisted forms as shadow expressions of a divine process within us. For me, creating a meaning-world is what it means to be human and created in the image of God. I cherish this gift now that I've recognized it more fully."

Other pastors experience the sacredness of world-making when threatened by its loss. We clergy know that persons suffering from conditions like Alzheimer's disease gradually lose their self—their sense of "I am . . . "—as they gradually lose their ability to constitute a stable reality. Indeed, individuals seem "dead" when they can no longer look out from where they are and create a place.

Some of us have been there. We remember vividly the fear of losing ourselves as our capacity to keep our world afloat began to slip away. And at times it did. Without the competency to make sense or to be sensible, we could not reconstitute ourselves; we could not hold on to any sense of who we were as persons. For a while in our depression, we died as we lost the ability to create a meaning-world around us.

Depression fractures our habitual awareness. It opens us to the awesome realization that being a self, and having a continuing sense of self, rests on the capacity to generate a cohesive meaning-world around us.

From this vantage point it is but a short step into the realm of the sacred. We are moved to affirm the blessedness of this capacity. We are filled with thanks for this holy gift when it returns to a loved one, or to us. Sacredness often reveals itself when we are threatened by the loss of its unexpected embodiments.

Filled with this sense of the sacred, our receptivity to meaning broadens:

We marvel at the new worlds of meaning which arise through the ongoing fractures in our thinking.

We honor even more the world-making efforts of others, even though we must confront their views at times.

We commit ourselves to cast off personal meanings that no longer fit us or are degrading to others.

We dedicate ourselves to form with others a supportive ring of intersubjective truth.

Our ability to create a meaning-world is Creator God's gift to humankind. And yet God becomes the Creator only when a meaning-world has been established by human consciousness. Through our depression we step beyond into sacred mysteries such as this.

SACRED BODY

"My body felt heavy when I was depressed," reminisced one pastor. "It was as if I had a weight pressing down on my shoulders, making me stagger along with each step. Maybe it was just the emotional weight on my heart, but whatever it was, I felt as if I were carrying my body instead of it carrying me."

"I was really upset after being told I needed medication for my chemical imbalance," recalled another pastor. "I moped around thinking that I was abnormal and that I would never feel strong and invincible again."

"I obsessed about my body when I was depressed," added a third clergyperson. "I worried about my eating, my sleeping, my sexual feelings, and even my bowels."

Depressed pastors are no longer light on their feet. Body movements are ponderous. Body functions falter. Body vitalities lose buoyancy. Body myths, of invincibility and the power to ward off death, plunge to the threshing floor. Gone are graceful rhythms, mighty strides, sweeping gestures, and victory dances. The body feels like a dense clod of earth, without life, soon dust.

Earlier worries about the body may have contributed to the onset of depression, but once depressed, pastors become preoccupied with their bodies. They may seem oblivious to the body and its needs, but rarely is that the case. A complex web of fears and wishes leads to what looks like withdrawal from the body. Not even suicide attempts are consequences of disinterest towards one's body, but rather despondent reactions to the loss of body vitality and the hope it generates.

Abnormal sensitivity to the body can be agonizing. It can even be dangerous as the body is defensively ignored or mistreated. Nevertheless, a blessing may be elicited from this condition.

Most of us pastors are not alienated from our bodies. We embrace incarnational theology and respect the realities of the body-mind connection. But many of us lack depth in living fully through our bodies. We habitually take our bodies for granted unless attending to them biologically or medically.

Depression can fracture the habituality of our body-consciousness. Body symptoms, medical diagnoses, disrupted physical relationships with others, inescapable sensations, and yearnings for restored body health can impress upon us the fuller nature of our embodied existence. By causing us to be preoccupied with our bodies, depression can break us open to new body-centered perceptions that become new dwelling places of the sacred.

"I wouldn't want to go through the same kind of heaviness I felt when I was depressed," continued the first pastor. "It was too much. But as I've struggled to gain something from this particular experience, I've caught hold of an understanding that I've not fully grasped before.

"It made me realize that my body grounds my existence. The thickness of my body is what gives me presence and substance. It's what holds me in the world. My sense of body weight, even in the form at times of physical sluggishness or heavyheartedness, counteracts the unbearable lightness of being that we humans are prone to feel—that sense that we are just fluff in a world blown by the winds of fortuitous events and irrevocable choices. There is something reassuring in the heaviness of my body. I feel more real and somehow more truthful when I'm fully in the flesh. I take it as God's way of anchoring my being—and even my character."

"My depression and diagnosis of chemical imbalance really shook me up," continued the second pastor. "It made me think about my death. The words *dust to dust* kept going over and over in my mind. That's what I was going to become, just dust. It was pretty scary.

"But as my depression lifted and I tried to look at these experiences with reverent imagination, the image of *dust to dust* began to change. I began to imagine how my dust is identical with the dust of everything else. My body substance and that of pets and plants and faraway stars are basically all the same. I am earthy brother and sister to all that lives and moves and has its being—dust to dust, dust with dust.

"This fellowship of common substance warms my heart. Through my body I am part of something larger than myself. I am part of the universe. There's a joy in thinking about that, and in the feeling that my body, everyone's body, is a sacred gift that links us firmly with others and with all of life."

"For a long time my depression circled upon itself," continued the third pastor. "The more I worried about my body the more depressed I became, which made me more worried about my body. Thank God, the spiral stopped. But that experience made me realize that while I can't let my body become my everything, nevertheless everything that I am, I am through my body.

"And so I'm trying now to live more *through* my body rather than be obsessively *in* my body. For example, I'm trying to make my religious life more body-centered. I intentionally take my body to church and worship through it. I pay attention to my feelings and body sensations and even try to enhance them as a way to communicate with God. I'm experimenting with ways to pray and create rituals that will lift up a sacred understanding of such biological functions as sleep, sexual desires, and even body eliminations. Our body, indeed, is the temple of God."

Just as through depression's fractures we were led to acknowledge the sacredness of life's particulars and the sacredness of our world-making, so, too, might we come to recognize the sacredness of our body.

When that happens, the joys of holy flesh are celebrated. Biological rhythms beating one with the universe are cherished. Our body as a holy vessel for experimenting with truth is exercised.

Our depression should launch searchings for our better self and for God. Stepping beyond is both a possibility and an obligation. Many of us approach it as a joyful invitation. There is life and more beyond depression. If you are not there yet, may anticipation sustain you.

CLOSING

A New Day

The *O Antiphons* are verses sung in the Roman Catholic Church before the Magnificat at Vespers or during the last week of Advent. The *O Oriens* lifts up this prayer:

> O Radiant Dawn, splendor of eternal light, sun of justice: come, shine on those who dwell in darkness and the shadow of death.[1]

God's illumination forever beckons us. It calls us out of our valley and into a new day. Let us do all we can to greet it.

NOTES

INTRODUCTION: HONORING OUR DEPRESSION

1. I have been minister of counseling at St. Peter's United Church of Christ, Elmhurst, Illinois for all my ministry.
2. The case examples throughout this book are either disguised accounts or illustrative narratives.

1. DIAGNOSING OUR DEPRESSION

1. The data on depression in this chapter have been gathered from current research articles and books. The "Implications for Clergy" are my own.
2. William E. Hulme, "Ministry in Depression," *The Journal of Pastoral Care* 48 (Spring, 1994): 91-94.
3. Susan Alloway, "Darkness Invisible," *Pastoral Psychology* 42 (November, 1993): 73-79.

2. DETERMINING HOW DEPRESSED WE ARE

1. Those familiar with my previous books will recognize this focus on levels of self-cohesion and self-disturbance. See especially, Robert L. Randall, *The Time of Your Life: Self/Time Management for Pastors* (Nashville: Abingdon Press, 1994).

4. OUR RENEWAL TASKS

1. C. Welton Gaddy, *A Soul Under Siege: Surviving Clergy Depression* (Louisville: Westminster/John Knox Press, 1991). This is an eloquent and frank account of his own depression and treatment.
2. William Hulme, "Ministry in Depression," *The Journal of Pastoral Care,* 48 (Spring, 1994): 91-94.
3. Thomas Moore, *Care of the Soul* (New York: Harper Perennial, 1992).

253.2
R189W

LINCOLN CHRISTIAN COLLEGE AND SEMINARY 93365

4. Leslie Brandt, *Psalms/Now* (St. Louis: Concordia Publishing House, 1973). Masculine pronouns referring to God have been deleted. Adapted with permission.
5. Ibid.
6. Ibid.
7. Ibid.

8. STEPPING BEYOND

1. Thornton Wilder, *Our Town* (New York: Harper & Row, 1985), 99. Used with permission.
2. Ibid., 100.

CLOSING: A NEW DAY

1. *Christian Prayer: The Liturgy of the Hours* (Collegeville, Minnesota: Liturgical Press, 1976), p. 90.

3 4711 00094 4159